SUSAN FERRARO

SWEET TALK

THE LANGUAGE OF LOVE

SIMON &
SCHUSTER
New York
London
Toronto
Sydney
Tokyo
Singapore

SIMON & SCHUSTER
Rockefeller Center
1230 Avenue of the Americas
New York, NY 10020

Designed by Pei Loi Koay

Cover design © 1994 by Janet Perr
Cover photo © by Erich Lessing / Art Resource
   (sculpture by Antonio Canova, *Psyche Brought
   Back to Life by the Kiss of Amour*)

Manufactured in the United States of America

10   9   8   7   6   5   4   3   2   1

Library of Congress Cataloging-in-Publication Data
Ferraro, Susan.
       Sweet Talk / by Susan Ferraro.
           p.   cm.
       Includes bibliographical references.
       1. English language—Lexicology. 2. Love—
Terminology. I. Title.
   PE1583.F47   1995
   423'.028—dc20   94-38386
                                                       CIP

ISBN 0-671-79234-2

ACKNOWLEDGMENTS

WRITERS ARE PRESUMPTUOUS CREATURES and get by, most often, by asking a lot of favors; I am no exception and wish to thank here the many friends and experts who contributed to *Sweet Talk.* Molly Friedrich, my agent, served as general and soldier both in what was a longer campaign than either of us imagined; she put words to my feelings when I could not with astonishing clarity. Rebecca Saletan taught invaluable lessons of prose and publishing, and on more than one occasion saved me from what must be the amorist's occupational hazard of excess. I am blessed with friends who contributed examples, stories, suggestions, and encouragement: Shirley and Pete Longshore, Don Harrison, Rhoda Gilinsky, Jim Schermerhorn, Carmen Cole and Dick Holt, Rebecca Shiffman and Fred Terna, Mae Sokol, Beth and Ricky Harrison, Betty Knoop, Elaine Marks, Lollo Meyer, Eva Sherman, Lois Slater, Allan Gold, Carmella Siconolfi, Florie Stickney, Margot Slade, Jack Stadler,

G. Blakemore Evans, Sara Paretsky, Sheri Holman and Denise Roy, Dan Buck, Bonnie Lewis, Vickie Gordon, Anna Lyons Roost, Jim Longshore, Charlotte Smirnoff, Murray Suid, Anne and Steve Markowski, Dana Ralls, John Wheatcroft, Joe Ferraro, Marina Ferraro, Matthew Ferraro, Tanya Didascalou, Julie Davidson, Kathleen Dill, Kathleen Mac-Namara, Scott Barton, Ann Dukes, Audrey Topping, Barbara MacDonald, Jeff Murphy, and several who choose to remain Anonymous.

for Joe, for always

for Professor G. Blakemore Evans,
a civilizing influence—scholarly, modest, impeccable, kind

and in memory of Ralynn Stadler,
a glittering Helen of the twentieth century, who first
suggested a book of love words

X O X O X O X O X O X O X

And now the happy season once more fits
That love-sick Love by pleading may be blest;
   For lovers say, the heart hath treble wrong
   When it is barr'd the aidance of the tongue.

WILLIAM SHAKESPEARE

VENUS AND ADONIS, *327–330*

X   *O*   X   *O*   X   *O*   X   *O*   X   *O*   X   *O*

CONTENTS

X O X O X O X O X O X O

INTRODUCTION
Sweet Nothings
That Mean
Everything

ONCE UPON A TIME I got married. It was a hastily planned event, because we couldn't stand not being married one more minute, but we pretty much covered the bases: Engraved invitations on creamy white paper. Church, license, blood tests. For him: new suit, new tie, haircut a week in advance so it wouldn't look too short. For me: white dress, white shoes, veil. Airplane tickets to and from my hometown. And a chat with the priest, an ethereal-looking cleric, who shook his finger in our faces and told us we would say "I *will*," not "I *do*," a word choice that began to make sense about a decade later, when I realized that *do* is for now, this minute, this day, but *will* is for a future unending.

The morning of the wedding was cool but bright, as December days often are in Northern California. I wasn't nervous, not really, and he was on time. Yes, I forgot the lovely train that hooked onto the back of my dress, and in rushing through the parish house to the chapel I more or less crashed the receiving line of another wedding. But we remembered to say *will,* not *do,* my voice was firm, his shook, and it was perfect.

Except that the whole thing took eleven minutes.

I remember, immediately afterward, standing outside the church, feeling not exactly stunned but startled. A gust of wind caught my veil and sent it shooting straight up, like a white tornado rooted to my skull (a moment caught for posterity by a friend with a camera). My eyes met my husband's.

"We're married," I said.

"I know," he said.

"It would take six months of legal wrangling to undo what it took eleven minutes to say in there," I said.

"I know," he said.

And at that moment the priest arrived, waving the marriage certificate, and we both signed it without hesitating even one second. But I knew then: language and love, both of them invisible and intangible, are potent stuff. A mere handful of syllables, uttered in certain places at certain times, changed us forever. He'd asked me to dance. He'd asked me out. He'd asked me to marry him. Yes, yes, yes, I'd said. Somewhere in there we had said the magic word *love.* I was first, and I whispered it, because I was afraid I'd scare him away, right out of my life. It was just a word, but it could have done that.

This book is a compendium and commentary on words of love, be they soft and tender, hot or edgy, comforting or demanding. It gives full weight to feelings. As Isaac Bashevis Singer once said, when literature "begins to ignore the passions, the emotions—it becoms sterile, silly and actually without substance." These are the words we humans BREATHE, CONFIDE, LISP, MOUTH, PROCLAIM, SAY, SHOUT FROM THE ROOFTOPS, SWEAR, UTTER LONGINGLY and RAPTUROUSLY, and WHISPER with the greatest personal fervor, and for all their inexactitude they deserve respect.

They don't get it very often. The truth is, we don't trust love words: it's no accident we call them SWEET NOTHINGS.

For one thing, love itself is a dubious, dangerous venture. It usually makes us feel crazy—as in I'M JUST CRAZY ABOUT YOU!—or, as the Greek lyric poet Anacreon wrote in the sixth century B.C., "I both love and do not love, and am mad and am not mad." Love makes us do stupid things, puts us at risk. It defies common sense. It laughs like a crazed romantic in the face of present danger, shrugs off the future, and yawns at the past. Love is oxymoronic, an unnecessary need, desirable yet burning, clear but puzzling. Not only can it pull the props right out from under intelligent behavior, it can even kill you. (If you don't believe this, consider all the precipitous heights named "Lovers' Leap.") A lover may be the worst possible choice—a deadbeat, an emotional albatross, a user, and a cad—and an entranced admirer, knowing all that, *still* loves him. Or her.

This is bad news. In the grand scheme of things, humans are puny beasts, thin-skinned and hairless, bereft of brawn, slow, clumsy, and stiff. But we have large brains, those quirky, individual engines of flesh, and the ability to speak, a fortuitous talent made possible by an ingenious arrangement of tongue, teeth, and windpipe. Darting to and fro between hormones and synapses, our capacity to love channeled through speech can sweeten life with pure joy—or ruin everything.

Also suspect is the link between love and sex. Our biological imperative (something we do share with other animals) is a worm nestled amid the roses of romance. Sex may even be the evolutionary *raison d'être* of love that prettified what must have been, back among the cavemen, pretty rough stuff. Alexander Pope said that "gentle love" is but "lust thro' some certain strainers." If romance is just a cosmetic makeover of primal urges, are love words the "certain strainers," the stuff rational creatures call pure hogwash? Maybe.

Finally, language itself doesn't quite mesh with love. Like logic, speech is supposed to follow rules; it's a system of specific meanings, order, and connections. Given that love is inexact, changeable, and inexpressibly sublime, we have to ask: Is it even possible to articulate feeling? Can we trust someone who does? As sincere as love language may seem—as true as it may be at the moment it is voiced or written—the emotion that inspires it can dry up, fade away, crumble

like an autumn leaf, and *we don't know why.* Disenchantment
among the lovelorn may amount to a mere scratch of experi-
ence, or it can be a searing, lifelong wound.

In Shakespeare's *Henry V,* the handsome, virile, ambitious
young king talks up a storm of love language while insist-
ing that he has no gift for pitching verbal woo:

> *"I know no ways to mince it in love, but directly to say, 'I
> love you.'. . . And while thou liv'st, dear Kate, take a fel-
> low of plain and uncoined constancy, for he perforce must
> do thee right, because he hath not the gift to woo in other
> places. For these fellows of infinite tongue that can rhyme
> themselves into ladies' favours, they do always reason
> themselves out again. What! A speaker is but a prater;
> . . . but a good heart, Kate, is the sun and the moon; or
> rather, the sun, and not the moon, for it shines bright and
> never changes, but keeps his course truly."*
>
> —V, ii, 128–170

Hogwash or pure heaven? Can a princess believe a king who
scoffs at those who weave love wreaths of words and then
proceeds to do just that? Even if he means it, will it last?
Humans are gabby, competitive, acquisitive; our great
brains too often settle for easy, temporary solutions. Some-
times we lie, even to ourselves.

The truth is that Kate will have to take her chances. She will have to sort out, as must we all, CUNNING SEDUCTION from HEARTFELT YAMMERING. Lovers POUR OUT THEIR HEARTS and WRITE REAMS and SERIOUSLY DIALOGUE and SHARE FEELINGS and RUN OFF AT THE MOUTH about love, and do all of it incessantly. Language may be hard-pressed when the subject is the heart, but it's indispensable: lovers both *do* and *will* talk about love—a lot.

For all its limitations and our doubts, language sometimes works for love: we describe feelings, organize them, and search for a way to satisfy ourselves without getting too hurt. For many of us love would not be love without the sweet murmur, and later analysis, of sweet nothings. Still, the vocabulary we've contrived for it is a hit-or-miss affair of contradiction and senselessness. For instance, in love talk diminutives signal grand, large feelings (MY DEAREST SWEETKINS). Baby talk announces strictly adult admiration (WHATTA BABE). We concoct logical impossibilities (HONEY BUNCH) and dress them up in nonsensical superlatives (MY GREATEST LITTLE DARLING). We call each other foodstuffs (SUGAR) and play at insults (YOU ADORABLE IDIOT!).

In short, endearments are familiar but specialized—forever yours and mine, forever full of what linguists of logic and law call "stipulated definitions," or phrases qualified by "private understanding." Strip away the polysyllabic abstracts, and what remain are words that mean more because everyone knows they must. In this context, "private understanding" can mean AFFIANCED, BETROTHED, ENGAGED, MATCHED, PAIRED OFF, PROMISED, or maybe just FOOLING AROUND.

Every book is a journey, for writer and reader alike. As I've collected and sorted love words, a project that grew and multiplied like love itself, I made discoveries. One was that everybody wants to make love, but nobody—not since the dawn of poetical time—knows what to make *of* love. Ovid likened it to warfare; he was banished from Rome because of his salacious and specific love lyrics in *Ars Amatoria* (and perhaps, too, for putting an amorous arm on the sister of the Emperor Augustus). Younger, more supercilious, possibly more gifted, Catullus was caught by unrequited love and wailed *Odi et amo,* "I hate and I love," which pretty much sums up love *in extremis.*

The passage of time did not bring wisdom: medieval poets got no further than two separate, unsettling statements from Chaucer: "Love Conquers All" was wishful thinking at its best; "Love Is Blind" is still the final, utterly feeble philosophical refuge for mothers who cannot understand why their daughters swoon over hoodlums. The Renaissance poet Samuel Daniel said love was a "sickness, full of woes," and many agreed, even if the chief symptom of the disease seemed to be glorious love sonnets by Shakespeare, Sir Philip Sidney, Edmund Spenser, Michael Drayton, and dozens of others, including the dour Daniel himself, who wrote his for Delia, an anagram for the word *ideal.*

And the twentieth century? Edna St. Vincent Millay rightly reasoned that

> *Love is not all: it is not meat nor drink*
> *Nor slumber nor a roof against the rain . . .*

but the Beatles made "All You Need Is Love" a hit single. Robert Graves, however, was still counting "symptoms of love" when he wrote, "Love is a universal migraine." The Spanish proverb *Quién bien te quiere te hara lloror* sums up the problem: "Whoever really loves you will make you cry." Great.

Another thing about endearments is that, deep in their etymological bones, a lot of them reflect our can't-live-with-it-can't-live-without-it ambivalence toward love; these supple, silken syllables reveal themselves to be full of duplicity, danger, and double meanings. Consider the word LOVE itself: *Webster's Ninth New Collegiate Dictionary* says that the Old English verb *lufu,* from which *love* derives, is "akin" (in the word business, as in love, relationships abound) to the Old High German word *luba,* meaning "love," and *luba* is from the Old English *leof,* or "dear." So far, so sweet. But *leof,* like an aging courtesan, has a history; it's from the Latin *lubere, libere,* "to please," and leads straight to the indispensable *libido,* defined as "primitive, biological urges." Moreover, back at the starting gate, the word *lufu* also connects with the Sanskrit word *lubh,* and it too means "desire."

DEAR, meaning "precious," may be the most common endearment between husbands and wives. Yet—oh dear—it also means "costly" or "painful." DELIGHT comes from the Latin root word *delicere,* "to allure," and once again—if we are lured under false pretenses—suggests subterfuge or connivance, either of which can lead to ruin. FANCY means love and attraction, as in this song in *The Merchant of Venice:*

> *Tell me, where is fancy bred,*
> *Or in the heart, or in the head?*
>
> *(III, ii, 63–64)*

It also means expensive. INTRIGUE shimmers with mystery, fascination, and allure—but its root is the Latin *intricare,* "to entangle," and it connects to *tricae,* or hair. Engage in romantic intrigue all you want, but one man's silken locks may be another's snarl. RAPTURE means ecstasy, joy, delight, transport, and bliss, which is curious; its Latin root is *rapere,* "to seize," which also happens to be the root of the word *rape.*

As first-year Latin students and crossword-puzzle aficionados know, AMOROUS comes from the Latin *amor;* in myth, Amor is the Roman name for the Greek Eros, the boyish, babyish embodiment of physical love. His mother, Venus, never identified his father; however, we know she was married to Vulcan, enjoyed stolen moments with mortals (among them the beautiful, doomed Adonis and the Trojan Anchises, by whom she had Aeneas), and consorted shamelessly with Mars, Zeus, and Hermes.

Sieved through French and Italian, *amor* gets around almost as much: there's AMOUR (lover), AMOUR-PROPRE (self-esteem), AMORETTO (a love cherub), and AMORIST (a devotee of love or—gentle reader, take note!—"one who writes of love"). Amor was also called Cupido; in time he became the little winged cherub who appears on Valentine's Day cards. He also provides the root word of CUPIDITY, or greed—the nasty, flip side of desire.

And so it goes in love language. A beautiful woman may be an irresistible SIREN, even SYLPHlike in form, and that's a compliment—except when it isn't. In the *Odyssey,* a Siren is a creature half bird, half woman, whose seductive melodies drive sailors mad and make them drown themselves. Sylphs meanwhile emerge etymologically from the Greek word for beetle or, yuckier still, larvae; they don't turn seductive until the Middle Ages, when Paracelsus describes them as elemental spirits. Today's sirens are still DROP-DEAD GORGEOUS (think about that phrase for a second), while contemporary sylphs are slim, sexy, and suckers for the latest in aerobics.

The miracle of all this—and for me the most delicious discovery of all about love language—is that many of the endearments we use today have been handed down from lovers of centuries past unchanged in meaning or even exact wording. Love is a place people have tended TO FALL INTO, as if it were a pillow or a pit, since 1423. Courting couples have been IN LOVE since 1508 at least, and they've wanted to MAKE LOVE since 1580.

Catullus hated and loved at the same time? I know just what he meant. Moderns still brood over the same imponderables: Does he love me? Will she be mine? Why did he hurt me so? Who can understand her? Why do I care? Why is this person as necessary to me as the breath I breathe, as essential as a cool drink of water in the hot desert of loneliness, as inevitable and exhausting as romantic hyperbole? Here's the famous Romantic poet Shelley:

> *What is love? Ask him who lives, what is life? ask him who adores, what is God? . . . if we feel, we would that another's nerves should vibrate to our own, that the beams of their eyes should kindle at once and mix and melt into our own, that lips of motionless ice should not reply to lips quivering and burning with the heart's best blood. This is love.*

And here, to me even more compelling, is a letter from the unfamous Caleb Hyatt, a Manhattan civil engineer, husband, and father, who took time after work one night to write his wife.

Sept. 16th. 1915.

My Dear Lady:

I think that before I turn in I will {write} you a sample of the work of my pretty new typewriter. She is certainly some peach. I was very sorry not to be able to come over this evening. I was however successful in finishing up this week's work for Father—for this I am very glad. Took Waldo to White Plains with me but did not get back until after nine.

I am very thankful that you are almost ready to come out and play with us once more. I take this opportunity to officially announce to you that it is very lonesome around here without you. And that your love and sweet self are most terribly needed by us. I love you dear heart and want you more than type can tell.

Further I wish to thank you for the dearest little girl in all the world. She is a little wonder to have won our hearts in only a four days' visit, but she most certainly can have me. Dearest Elvira and dear little "Sally," good night.

Your loving husband & father
Caleb.

That we speak and write of love so often does not make it easy. In *Clea,* the final novel in Lawrence Durrell's *Alexandria Quartet,* the writer confronts the problem of love language head-on:

I am hunting for metaphors which might convey some-thing of the piercing happiness too seldom granted to those who love; but words, which were first invented against de-spair, are too crude to mirror the properties of something so profoundly at peace with itself, at one with itself. Words are the mirrors of our discontents merely; they contain all the huge unhatched eggs of the world's sorrows. Unless perhaps it were simpler to repeat under one's breath some lines torn from a Greek poem, written once in the shadow of a sail, on a thirsty promontory in Byzantium. Some-thing like . . .

> *Black bread, clear water, blue air.*
> *Calm throat incomparably fair.*
> *Mind folded upon mind*
> *Eyes softly closed on eyes.*
> *Lashes a-tremble, bodies bare.*

BOOK *III,* CHAPTER 2

We know that the word *love* alone usually isn't enough; even Ferdinand felt compelled to embroider his love for Miranda in *The Tempest:* ". . . I/Beyond all limit of what else i' th' world,/Do love, prize, honour you." Partly this is because, as Richard Lederer points out in *The Miracle of Language,* the word is overused: "We love our parents and children; we love our spouses and paramours. We love our country; we love country music. We love God; we love our new hat. We love *The Iliad;* we love *Love Story. Love* has become such a do-it-all convenience word that it debases the emotion that is so resonant with infinite variety."

Yet oddly enough, in this area of human experience, quantity somehow proves quality. For starters, love comes in so many different models: PLATONIC (a theoretical state, alleged by philosophers and those said to be just good friends, but rarely glimpsed in a natural habitat), CHIVALRIC, ROMANTIC, PARENTAL, PATRIOTIC, EROTIC, SELFISH and SELF-SACRIFICING, CONJUGAL and COITAL or SEXUAL. Its effect, too, is so various; as Joshua Poole, author of *The English Parnassus* in 1677 noted, love can be IMPERIOUS, MELTING, FAWNING, WANTON, LASCIVIOUS, and SLIPPERY —although my favorites in his lengthy word list are the terrifying MARROW-BOILING, the all-too-vivid JEALOUS-WINGED, and the alarming THIEVISH, ITCHING, FRIZZLED, CRISPED, SLEEK-HAIRED, and EYE-RAVISHED. Like love itself, the words of love are often not enough or too much.

Yet in love, as in art, we know what we like. Endearments taken and given with good intention, in the everyday fields of affection and desire, comprise a brave, gentle lingo. When Tina Turner wants to know "What's love got to do with it?" I want to tell her: Love has everything to do with it, and love language—that stuff we casually dismiss as SWEET TALK—is the means.

So what if our words never quite meet the challenge of defining love and feeling? So what if we make fools of ourselves now and then? Love language may sound silly, but it is vocabulary and art built on trust, with fingers irrationally but resolutely crossed. It reveals an imaginative playground—funny, delightful, alluring, encouraging, shamelessly incredible, nonplused, and infinitely mysterious, because love is real magic. If Anton Chekhov could call the woman he desired a "Doggie, my dear puppy," we might do the same, or substitute something even sillier, like "My sweet patootie."

And what is a PATOOTIE, sweet or otherwise? To begin your discovery, turn the page.

THE ALPHABET
OF LOVE

UST HOW DIFFERENT is the language of love? For most, it's everyday parlance heard through sweetly humming earphones (the aural equivalent, I suggest, of rose-colored glasses)—a verbal simper refined by a glance, breathed through a sigh, smacking at last with the satisfaction of big, big kisses and rows of exclamation points. One thing is sure: we know love words when we hear them.

Consider CUTE: American women of all ages use it to describe a man or boy who is attractive and (potentially, at least) lovable. *Webster's Ninth,* however, has this to say about CUTE:

> {short for *acute*} (1731) 1: CLEVER, SHREWD 2: attractive or pretty esp. in a dainty or delicate way 3: obviously straining for effect.

The first definition sounds like what everyone wants—in a lawyer, not a lover. *Attractive* is good, but *pretty, dainty,* and

delicate are not what women mean when they sigh (or ex-
claim, as the case may be), "That guy is *soooo* cute"—that
cute means *fascinating, sexy, alive.* To wit: in October 1992, a
young woman, when asked by *The New York Times* why she
supported Bill Clinton, said, "Because he's young and he's
cute." Clinton may be many things to many people, but he
is not *pretty, dainty,* or *delicate.* But we know what she
meant, or at least what she thought she meant.

Love is arbitrary and expansive, and so am I: the basic,
start-up Vocabulary of Love—the *ne plus ultra* word list for
ROMANCE and FLIRTATION and DEVOTION, the words guar-
anteed to provide safe passage into if not through the little-
known territories of Passionate Affection—can be contained
in an alphabet of no more than one essential, established,
but evocative word for each letter. That's the arbitrary part,
and here's what's expansive: included also, strictly for the
sake of clarification and because it *feels* right, are kissing
cousins—smitten synonyms, if you will—on both the deno-
tative and connotative sides of the family. The designated
essential utterances are mostly nouns, but allow for a fair
sprinkling of vital verbs and rousing adjectives.

A is for ardor, always, but the endearment that leads the A-team of lovespeak is ANGEL. Its family tree makes the Windsors look like parvenus: *angel,* meaning messenger from God, comes from Old English *engel* by way of Old French *angele,* mixed with a Teutonic adaptation of a Latin translation, *angelus,* of the late Hebrew *mal'ak* (full form, *mal'ak yehouwah*), and also connected to the Greek *angelos.* *Angelic* lovers are *heavenly,* often suffused in a halo of light, and even a shade *saintly* (though that quality can obstruct earthly union and is best, in the best of all real worlds, not pursued). Angels *guide, minister, tend, nurture, rescue, protect,* and most of all earn our adoration because they *adore* mere mortals.

There are, officially, nine orders of angels, including cherubim, also known as *putti* in Italian. (Don't confuse one of these, ever, with a *puta,* an elided form of *putane,* Italian slang for whore. *Pasta putanesca* may be heavenly, especially if it's made with angel-hair pasta, but according to folklore still current in Italian homes it's an earthy dish with a sauce of leftovers hastily thrown together, right before the man of the house gets home, by a woman who has been up to no good.)

When you call your love an angel, you reach back

through four hundred years of sweet compliment and hope to the moment when Edmund Spenser idealized a woman's "angel's face" in *The Faerie Queene.* You connect with almost every culture, on every tier of society; the last Czarina of Russia addressed letters to Czar Nicolas II, "My own dearest Angel." (In reply, he simpered this nauseating closing: "Your poor little weak-willed hubby"—not at all heavenly but probably too, too true.)

Mutual adoration aside, why angels? Milton drops hints of the pleasurable commingling of delicately blushing spirits in *Paradise Lost,* but for the unwinged masses they remain hard to grasp: ephemeral, wisps of gossamer and smoke, too often animated by self-righteousness and moral superiority. Still, love is part idealization: " 'Tis strange what a man may do, and a woman yet think him an angel," mused William Makepeace Thackeray in *Henry Esmond.* And with no corporeal substance, angels have selflessness down pat. Wrote Alphonse de Lamartine, a French poet and statesman, in a nineteenth-century novel called *Graziella,* "To love for the sake of being loved is human, but to love for the sake of loving is angelic." We want that love. We want it free.

I sleep, but my heart waketh: it is the voice of my beloved
that knocketh, saying, Open to me, my sister, my love, my
dove, my undefiled.

—SONG OF SONGS, 5:2.

BELOVED is a respectful, selfless endearment, old-fashioned,
somewhat formal but not yet creaking, though it dates from
1526. The word attained a worshipful intensity in the nine-
teenth century among the Romantics and even a few Victo-
rians. Robert Browning wrote in "Life in a Love," in 1855:

> *Escape me?*
> *Never—*
> *Beloved!*
> *While I am I, and you are you.*

A *lover* is an equal, but one who is *beloved* has magical pow-
ers, or perhaps is wondrously perfect. Like beauty, *belovedness*
is in the eye of the beholder. In *De l'Amour,* written in 1822,
Stendhal talked about "that action of the mind that discov-
ers fresh perfections in its beloved at every turn of events."

$\mathscr{C}$

Unlike an angel, a CATCH is materially tangible, somebody
you can get your hands on, if you're lucky, because he, or
she, is blessed with great assets like beauty or, even better,
great bankable bounty otherwise known as wealth. A *catch*
is also a LIKELY PROSPECT, someone who might be (*should* be,
in the eyes of most mothers) nailed to the wall of matri-
mony (or a prom dance list, depending on your social calen-
dar). Slangy qualifiers dog contemporary usage—*a real,* or
some, or *quite a,* or *what a catch*—but the term has a formida-
ble history as a verb of amorous angling. In *Antony and
Cleopatra,* Caesar says of the dead queen,

> *but she looks like sleep,*
> *As she would catch another Antony*
> *In her strong toil of grace.*

> *(V, ii, 349)*

Landing the right catch entails mutual understanding, known
today as COMMITMENT, three tough, tight syllables that too
often front soft thinking and insufficient feeling. Popular-
ized in the 1980s, this lugubrious word tries to go love one
better, beyond mere devotion to a *willingness to commit.*
Maybe. When I was growing up, *commitment* was what self-

righteous, irritable adults did to somebody near and undear when they checked her into the nuthatch, and in any event it connotes contracts, obligations, duty. It's true that people in love often feel crazy, and marriage is a contract that can, when the parties stop partying, end up in court. But *commitment* is not delightful. It's a serious, studied word, a topic for debate and logical resolution, a bore. If you intend *to commit to a relationship,* forget the flowers, and get out the legal pads to start listing pros and cons.

Ah, RELATIONSHIP: another ugly, awkward love word, without which no modern lover can sally forth. It's useful, I suspect, because it doesn't mean much; *relationships* can range from hand-holding to torrid sex—no one, including the participants, need know exactly what is meant, though people are more and more likely to KISS AND TELL these days (often on a nationally syndicated talk show). The difference between RELATIONSHIP and the almost equally vague GET INVOLVED is that the former is verbally closer, or *relates well,* to *relatives,* thus suggesting an implicit family *commitment,* whereas the latter always means sex.

D

The Old French word *deore* is the source for the quintessential endearment DEAR, and its close relations DEAREST and DARLING—almost interchangeable words for those we *cherish, favor, adore,* and often linked romantically with the alliterative *delight* and *desire.* In use since the twelfth century, *darling* is the oldest; true to its origins, it was sometimes spelled *dearling* through the eighteenth century. It can be silly or sentimental, fine stuff or coarse, an appellation for the mistress of the boudoir or the name of the adorable young dog owner in Disney's *Lady and the Tramp.* It is always familiar, a complimentary presumption, as in Henry Carey's 1729 rhyme "Sally in Our Alley":

> *Of all the girls that are so smart,*
> *There's none like pretty Sally.*
> *She is the darling of my heart,*
> *And she lives in our alley.*

The more frequent *dear* and its superlative *dearest* came into use about 1400; that which is *dear* is *precious, rare, glorious, worthy*—a jewel, or joy itself. To lose something precious is to suffer a *dear loss.* Overuse has cheapened its value: waitresses, doctors, and men trying to be helpful at the self-serve gas station call strangers *dear;* businessmen with anything but love on their minds have been using *Dear* as an opening salutation in letters since 1450. (For someone who really *is* dear to me, I often begin *"Dear, dear"* for in true affection redundancy is no sin.) DEARIE is low class but well intentioned—unless, of course, a poet latches hold as Robert Burns did in 1792, in "Highland Mary," and breaks your heart:

> *The golden hours on angel wings*
> *Flew o'er me and my dearie;*
> *For dear to me as light and life*
> *Was my sweet Highland Mary.*

Pity the poor ENCHANTRESS: like Jessica Rabbit in the movie *Who Framed Roger Rabbit,* she's not bad, she's just *drawn* that way. So are her sisters in sorcery, *sylphs, sirens,* and *witches.* If it's true that literature imitates life, the world must be full of beautiful bad women, and fuller still of men who just can't help being scared, possessed, dragged to their doom and beyond by *femmes fatales* who intoxicate the poor guys with irresistible sexual charm while *casting spells* that lead to ruin.

Or that's what they say the next day; I think it's all sexual politics and power games, that the luxury of allure outweighs the inescapable force every time. For what it's worth, however, "wicked women"—from Circe, whose magic wine turned men into pigs, to the Eagles' "Witchy Woman"—have been an excuse for men's riotous escapades, sybaritic excesses, and plain old flings.

Young girls are *enchanting,* and that's a compliment: tempered by youth and innocence, their kind of allure is socially acceptable. Still, they bear watching—give them a few years and they too may become *experienced* mistresses of magic and seduction:

> *Tell me not here, it needs not saying,*
> *What tune the enchantress plays*
> *In aftermaths of soft September*
> *Or under blanching mays,*
> *For she and I were long acquainted*
> *And I knew all her ways.*

> —*A. E. HOUSMAN, 1922*

If an enchantress and her cohort trade in the supernatural, FLIRTS are strictly terrestrial, and small-time too: they play the game for fun and flattery, not Fate. At the time of Elizabeth I, the verb *to flirt* meant *to flick,* as a lady might a fan (over which she might also cast engaging, provocative glances); the most likely source is the Anglo-Saxon *fleardian,* meaning a trifle, and a *flirt* often *trifles* with another's affections. *Flirting* is unisex—in John Gay's play *The Distress'd Wife,* in 1732, a *flirt* is "one who gives himself all the airs of making love in public"—but more opprobrium attaches to the female of the species. (Males just can't help themselves; see ENCHANTRESS, above.)

A particularly dangerous *flirt* is an OLD FLAME—the uninvited guest at the wedding or class reunion who knows exactly how to *light a fire,* or *ignite passion,* and *which match to strike.* If still *carrying a torch* for old time's satiation, he (but again, more likely she) can be vindictive: hell hath no fury like an intimate exiled. Those who kindle new love often fear *old flames* inordinately: even when they've banked their fires, they know too much, they know *more.*

Some *flirts,* females only and best viewed in soft focus, are COQUETTES. They can be found giggling, winking, and pouting their way through Regency novels, Harlequin Romances, the courts (regal and athletic) of the rich and famous, private affairs, and the vast reaches of their own mirrored reflections—usually in the powder room of someone else's house. An unpleasant falseness is innate, however adorable the contrivance: the *American Heritage Dictionary* traces the word to the Latin *coco,* meaning "a cackling, of imitative origin." More directly, as Joseph T. Shipley observes, the word came into English from the French *coq*— the rooster, a presumptuous fowl who struts, preens, and crows for the sake of crowing. *Coquettes* are more annoying than dangerous, although the contributor who defined the word for *The Oxford English Dictionary* may have had a more personal and painful experience of the type: "A woman (more or less young), who uses arts to gain the admiration and affection of men, mainly for the gratification of vanity and or from a desire of conquest, and without any intention of responding to the feelings aroused; a woman who habitually trifles with the affections of men, a flirt."

To be fair: in times of crisis—when the ship is sinking and there's no other boat in sight—*coquettes* can distract and inspire, and though it's unusual, the word can do a verb's job with conviction:

> *oh i should worry and fret*
> *death and i will coquette*

there's a dance in the old dame yet
toujours gai toujours gai

—*DON MARQUIS,*
THE SONG OF MEHITABEL, *1927*

An old (and much more affectionate) synonym is MINX, a pert, saucy girl, more adorable than alarming. Today's equivalent of *coquette,* TEASE, is sexual in implication but brings the word full circle in slang: a *cocktease* (*CT* for the well-bred and squeamish) is no one's idea of delight.

You might think, looking at GLAMOUR, that it's glitzy *amour,* the most exciting kind of romanticism—and you'd be right, at least in this century. Joseph Conrad used it that way in *Youth* in 1902: "Only a moment, a moment of strength, of romance, of glamour . . ." But three hundred years earlier, when Sir Walter Raleigh introduced *glamour* to English, it was a Scottish reworking of dusty, dull, rigorous *grammar*—that's right, the tedious rules of language. In those days, parts of speech shimmered with captivating magic, not because there was no TV and everyone had a longer attention span but because those who possessed "grammary" could make things happen by "practicing" secret knowledge (what we call reading). Today we have *Glamour* magazine, *glamour gals,* and anyone can be a *glamour puss* (that is, have a gorgeous face).

H

Hands are hot in John Donne's "The Ecstasy," but the HEART wins hands down as a love word. Two hearts beat in every working vocabulary: the four-valved pump of extraordinarily tough, reliable muscle that sends blood coursing through our bodies, and the delicate, quivering, easily touched and bruised core of our emotional being that we say determines delight or spells sadness. What the actual and the symbolic have in common is durability: real hearts go on beating long after the emotions have retired from the loving field, and the heart is ubiquitous in love talk. AFTER ONE'S OWN HEART has been in use in what became English since 825. *Hearts* have been *dear* and *sweet* since 1305, with *mie swete hurte* (an unintentional but telling pun); in 1350, *mi dere hert* appears. And we find this line in the earliest English comedy, Nicholas Udall's *Ralph Roister Doister* (1553): "Howe do thee sweete Custance, my heart of gold, tell me how?"

Should a surfeit of hearts cloy, consider this: the Greeks located the seat of the emotions in the liver. But other ancients disagreed, perhaps because the beating heart makes itself known: we can see it throb at a throat, feel it pound in our chests. Egyptian mummifiers left the heart in the body because they believed it was "indispensable" to the being; the Romans understood *cor,* the neuter noun meaning *heart,* to be "the seat of the feelings, the soul" (whereby Virgil writes *exsultantia corda*). Whole worlds and cultures away, the Chinese character for the word "love" has, in its center, the symbol for heart. The love connection is immediate, even *heartfelt:* hearts are necessary to life, so it's natural at those times when love seems greater than life itself that we feel compelled to GIVE OUR HEARTS or GAIN THE HEART of another; those we adore are, in slang, HEART THROBS.

The most common love word.

A JEWEL is a *joy, precious* in the best sense (at least in the eyes of the loving beholder), and sometimes but not necessarily a decoration. A jewel is never, however, *a trifling bauble,* but a sparkling character of finely faceted judgment, the stuff of pure, prized honor and astonished delight.

Courtly love was high concept in the Middle Ages, which meant that KNIGHTS took over the champion sweepstakes monopolized since the dawn of time by ancient HEROES. This was good if not great news for women: knights are heroes minus a literary lineage of classic warriors and cads like Achilles, who saw women as booty (any connection to the slang *booty* for buttocks is purely coincidental). It was a knight's job to do the right thing—seek the grail, serve his liege, honor and protect women. Modern *damsels in distress* still keep a lookout, somewhat wistfully, for a KNIGHT IN

SHINING ARMOR, or a KNIGHT ON A WHITE HORSE. And they are still the subject of ballads.

> *I am the knight who will fight for your honor,*
> *I am the hero that you're dreaming of.*

>   —*PETER CETERA,* 1989

It may have been only yesterday for *you,* but as long ago as 1225 a lover asserted, "He is my life and my love," or as *The Oxford English Dictionary* preserves it, "He is mi lif and mi luue." These are the moments, good and bad, when a lover feels that existence is meaningless, or perhaps just unimaginable, without the truest love, the one who regulates happiness by the lift of an eyebrow or the turn of a smile.

> *Thou art my life, my love, my heart,*
> *   The very eyes of me;*
> *And hast command of every part*
> *   To live and die for thee.*

>   —*ROBERT HERRICK, "TO ANTHEA, WHO*
>   *MAY COMMAND HIM ANYTHING"*

For others, life only begins when love arrives.

> *Because the birthday of my life*
> *Is come, my love is come to me.*

—*"A BIRTHDAY," CHRISTINA*
GEORGINA ROSSETTI, 1862

And me? I agree.

MAMA, a love term for adult women, is less an Oedipal-style Freudian slip than an earthy recognition of fully realized female power and attraction. DADDY, often a SUGAR DADDY, is old but rich; his pockets bulge with spare credit cards and trinkets from Tiffany's. In the musical *Gentlemen Prefer Blondes,* the appealing man-chaser Lorelei Lee explains everything in "Just a Little Girl from Little Rock" with the line: "The one you call your Daddy ain't your Pa."

In a barn, nuzzlers are horses with big, soft, whiskery noses, who want cubes of sugar. In a bed a NUZZLER is a warm, sometimes whiskery, often fresh, occasionally demanding, thoughtless *hugger,* an *embraceable you,* who feels free to be (just a little) animalistic. A CUDDLER is similar but less peremptory: to *coll* was to fondle in the arms in 1564; the pansy was called *cull-me-to-you,* and *cull* meant "gather." Women and lovers have been CUDDLESOME since 1863: "She was slender, and if one may so speak of a princess, she was cuddlesome!"

O!, the romantic spelling of OH!, was favored by the young and affected Romantic poets, and O is short for orgasm in pornographic literature. But in terms of true love language, OLD THING—a term for married lovers, longtime compan-ions, or lifelong friends—is the real thing, a British bit of sweet talk that has some currency in the United States, particularly among fans of *Masterpiece Theatre.*

PARAMOURS, on the other hand, are love objects of wild, leaping passions so great they soar above pedestrian social bonds (like marriage); as the Wife of Bath remarked of her penultimate spouse in 1365, "My fourth husband, he was a reveler, this is to say, he had a paramour." The word is kissed with French, fore and aft: *par* means *through* and *amour* is, as always, love. Of paramount importance, these significant other lovers occasionally drive themselves full circle into domesticity.

> *I sue not now thy Paramour to Bee*
> *But as a Husband, to be Link'd to thee.*
>
> —*MICHAEL DRAYTON,*
> *"HEROIC EPISTLES VII," 1598*

PARAGONS, often of virtue, are walking ideals, paramours viewed from afar; they are well advised to avoid being PUT ON A PEDESTAL where the air is thin and the comfort cool as marble.

The QUEEN of Love is Venus, or so Shakespeare thought, which is good enough for me; it's a commanding if rare love term. She can be A FAIRY QUEEN, a QUEEN OF THE NIGHT or OF PLEASURE. She is adult, dangerous, not always but sometimes kinky.

> *If you were queen of pleasure,*
> *And I were king of pain,*
> *We'd hunt down love together*
>
> *—ALGERNON SWINBURNE,*
> *"FAUSTINE," 1866*

In the Court of Love the QUEEN rules feelings, her subjects' hearts, and her family of *king, prince,* and *princess.*

ROMANCE does it all in love language. Of the five modern "Romance" languages—the linguistic descendants of Latin,

French, Italian, Spanish, Rumanian, and Portuguese—all but Rumanian are *romantic* in the modern sense: they give voice to cultures that seem passionate, emotional, and seriously happy about lovemaking. Some of this is national temperament, some of it literary coincidence; the earliest love stories of knights and ladies and magical events were written in Old French, or Provençal, and so came to be known as *romances.* The most famous, *Roman de la Rose,* was begun mid-twelfth century. In it, fantasy, coincidence, and visionary episodes made the emotionally surreal incongruities of bewitching love (a new idea in social relations) seem almost credible. It was a start, but no more: if sentiment had found a place, it wasn't promising, and love as we understand it today almost always led to disaster, war, frustration, or the unrequited loneliness of a convent cell, last refuge of royal sinners. Modern romances continue the literary tradition—unlikely events, exotic climes, handsome warrior heroes, secrets that can be ignored but not forgiven or vice versa—with two telling modifications: love takes center stage, and the damsel gets the star turn.

As a love verb, ROMANCE is synonymous with COURT and the more haphazard, primitive WOO; Shakespeare's unscrupulous Earl of Suffolk remarks of Henry VI's future wife:

> *She's beautiful and therefore to be woo'd;*
> *She is a woman, therefore to be won.*

—PART I, *V, iii,* 78

Personally, I prefer sex, but very well-paid experts on human behavior—among them Helen Gurley Brown, editor of *Cosmopolitan* magazine—have gone on record with the opinion that a good meal (one can only assume a *really* good meal) is better. Whichever you prefer, a person who is pleasing, delightful, kind, indulgent, and satisfying is SWEET, a SWEETHEART, a SWEETEST. *Sweets* of one kind or another have been cloying lovers' senses since the year 900, although in medieval days it was sometimes spelled *sweat,* which can be, if you're really gone on the guy, delectable. It's good news to know that the infatuated have been SWEET IN BED since 1300. In the early eighteenth century, the diminutive SWEETIE not only meant something like LUVIE, but a sweetmeat or a lollipop as well. A neglected variant that deserves revival is SWEETING, in healthy, frequent use as late as Colley Cibber's 1721 play *Rival Fools,* Act II: "Why, how now, sweeting—What a whole half-hour from me?" SWEETLING dates to 1648, a grandchild of SWEETIKIN, first used in 1599; the latter is inexplicably passé but has its charms in this sixteenth-century line from Thomas Nashe: "She is such a hony sweetikin."

In the 1930s, TOOTS emerged as an American slang term for an attractive or available woman, a MISTRESS—a friendly word if a bit fresh, a sassy endearment and perhaps the linguistic cousin, in some inexplicable way, of TOOTSIE WOOT-SIE, a bit of rhyming baby talk. TOOTSIES have been toddlers' toes since the eighteenth century; a lover might or might not offer to warm them up and a Latin scholar lover might amuse herself and her sweetheart with the word *tootsicum.* Slang expert Robert L. Chapman suggests that there may be some connection to the Yiddish phrase *zees tushele,* which means "sweet bottom" and appears as *tush* or *tushie* in contemporary affectionate American slang.

U is the short form of the second most common love word. I kid U not: find it and use it at the end of love letters—I Luv U.

A VALENTINE (rhymes with *be mine* in kindergarten classes and throughout life) is a sweetheart or a love token, both of which proliferate on February 14, St. Valentine's Day, when the shape of love is a full-bosomed, narrow-waisted "heart" hieroglyph the color of blood or passion, take your pick. (There are actually two St. Valentines, neither of whom had anything to do with love, but their saints' days coincide with an old Roman festival of birds, spring, flight, and other mating games.) Valentine hearts are everywhere: carved into tree trunks, scrawled in school notebooks, drawn and printed on bumper stickers and in slogans: I ❤ NEW YORK, I ❤ CATS, I ❤ MY VOLVO. Arrows often pierce these arty hearts, evidence that Cupid, blind but ambivalent Amor, has passed by and aimed true. Passionate lovers say they will die of a BROKEN HEART, and sometimes, like Cathy in *Wuthering Heights,* they do. Laugh if you must, but broken hearts are jagged halves, sometimes with a broken arrow sticking out at an odd angle.

The simplest, most common words mean the most if only WE listen closely. In Carson McCullers's dramatic adaptation of her novel *The Member of the Wedding,* the young heroine, Frankie, tells her even younger cousin, John Henry: "Not to belong to a 'we' makes you too lonesome."

In love notes, X is a kiss. Rows of Os are hugs. XOX2U!

Next time you find yourself YEARNING, relax in the sure knowledge that the word for your perplexing condition has one of the best-tended family trees in the language of love, so you're not alone (even if it feels that way). What's more, if you keep at it long enough you will find, like a jewel in the dust of ancient lexicography, joy. Working backward, then: English speakers have been *yearning* since before the twelfth century, when the Middle English *yernen* took over from Old English *giernan.* That word was related to Old High German *geron,* which meant "to desire," from the Latin *hortari,* "to urge and encourage." The joy part? *Hortari* connects to the Greek *chairein,* "to rejoice."

PINING and LONGING, HUNGERING and THIRSTING are insistent, biological synonyms, but a HANKERING is more superficial, even annoying—an *itch* perhaps. Similar in sound and spirit to both *yearn* and *hanker* is YEN, an American word since 1921—"I got a yen for you." It's cross-cultural in origin, derived from the Chinese word *yen yen,* or "opium craving" (itself derived from the Cantonese dialect *in-yan,* where *in* means "opium" and *yan* is "craving"). In speaking, *yen* is "yearn," with juice.

A ZZZZZZZ, the universal snore, is what a loved one is not.

♡♡

A LIST AS WE NOW KNOW IT is an abbreviated catalog, but actually the word is—yes!—romantic at its etymological heart. As a verb, LIST comes from Old English *lystan,* akin to *lust* (which means lust); in the Middle Ages, spelled *lysten,* it meant *to please* or *to suit.* As a noun, a thirteenth-century LIST was either a craving and inclination or, to practitioners of "manly" arts, a field of competition (among jousting knights *and* in the fields of chivalric love). LISTING means atilt, like a ship sailing difficult seas—an adjective all too fitting (should we somehow retain the wit to play the metaphor game while awash in the breaking tides of love) for those who navigate the oceans of emotion.

There are, then, the lists of Life—grocery lists and laundry lists—and the lists of Love, to wit:

TEN THINGS WE DO FOR LOVE

1. KISS

> *Jenny kissed me when we met*
> *Jumping from the chair she sat in;*
> *Time, you thief, who love to get*
> *Sweets into your list, put that in!*
> *Say I'm weary, say I'm sad,*
> *Say that health and wealth have missed me,*
> *Say I'm growing old, but add,*
> *Jenny kissed me.*

> —JAMES LEIGH HUNT
> ENGLISH JOURNALIST AND POET,
> 1784–1859

2. RENDEZVOUS

3. Throw a VALENTINE'S DAY party. The ancient Romans celebrated Lupercalia, a festival for Lupercus, a fertility god and cousin to the irresistible Pan, on

February 15. The party was—by modern standards—horrible: young men ran around slapping women with bloody thongs called *februa,* cut from the hides of sacrificed animals. Enter the Christians, who had two saints named Valentine. Neither had much to do with love, but February 14 was their name day and the day in late winter when, according to folklore, birds paired off for mating. One thing led to another, the parties crashed, and we have Valentine's Day—ideally with a box of chocolates and at least one red rose.

4. SPOON, DOTE ON, HANG ON EACH OTHER'S EVERY WORD

5. DRESS TO KILL

6. KILL

7. OGLE, LEER, GIVE THE GLAD EYE, HIT ON, MAKE A PASS AT

8. POP THE QUESTION

9. GET HITCHED

10. Write EPITHALAMIA, poems that celebrate wed-
dings. Sappho did it first, Catullus carried it for-
ward, Spenser made it sing in English, and despite
the complexity of its rhyme scheme, the form lives
on:

> *The man who made glum Athens laugh*
> *At itself told seriously what true*
> *Love is: Each one's not one but half*
> *In need of half. To make one from two*
>   *I marry you.*
>
> *Unlike those meteors that veer*
> *Dissonantly off on tangents, we*
> *Will make of our joined hemispheres*
> *A world of well-tuned harmony*
>   *When you wed me.*
>
> *Our marriage will be like a pair*
> *Of shears—no matter how far apart*
> *We're thrust, still we'll be joined. Don't dare*
> *Get caught in the blades' returning arc,*
>   *Outsiders! Dear heart,*

We know our flesh is contraband.
In muck and dreck we slip and sluther.
No way we can restore the land
To the far of our first sire and mother
    By marrying each other.

And yet the time of singing's come
We hear the voice of the turtledove
Though it's fall. This epithalamium
Marks both the end and commencement of
    Our wedding, Love.

    —*JOHN WHEATCROFT, ON THE*
    OCCASION OF HIS MARRIAGE
    TO KATHERINE WARNER,
    NOVEMBER 14, 1992

LOVE MODIFIED (NOT!)

IN THE VOCABULARY OF LOVE, adjectives and adverbs plied and piled atop endearments do not "modify" meaning, in the sense of reducing or mitigating it: quite the opposite. They intensify heartfelt utterances, and—with love so frequently given over to excess, body and soul—the quantity of qualifiers often weighs in as a sign of quality itself. Some of these happy intensifiers are ABSOLUTE, BRILLIANT, COMPLETE, FABULOUS, INCREDIBLE, SUPER, TOTAL, UTTERLY, and WILD.

But first, just who are these ever-loving companions who so inspire us? Linguists (and middle-aged singles) often bemoan the lack in English of an adequate word for what we mean when we say BOYFRIEND or GIRLFRIEND. Those words connote immaturity, not grown-up love play. What we want to say is something that means "a companion in amorous delights or intentions, including sexual passion and feeling." But "love interest" sounds more clinical than restorative, more a debit than an asset in the column of life's adventures. An AMORIST is "a devotee of love, a gallant," but no one uses it much these days. YOUNGHEDE, which meant boyfriend around 1300 and was recently unearthed by language archaeologist Susan Kelz Sperling, has been inexplicably abandoned. So the words BOYFRIEND and GIRLFRIEND still leap twixt lips, whether the lovers are 12 or 112. And they are also the usual terms for live-in lovers, people who share the same home and bed but are not married.

Those who would prefer to say it otherwise include the erudite and gentlemanly Richard Lederer. In *The Miracle of Language,* he cites San Francisco columnist Herb Caen's suggestion of UMMER (a neologism that fills the pause while a parent explains the unmarried state of a child's bliss, as in "And this is Roger, my daughter's um, er . . ."). Lederer himself, who committed (as he phrased it) "an act of public matrimony" in 1991, favors COVIVANT for those living together in a love relationship, a word he tracks to the late 1970s. It implies, he says, intimacy, "cohabitual accuracy," sexual equality, and what can be summed up as pleasing energy. It hasn't gained a large following, though. Perhaps the *co* sounds more corporate than corporeal. My own preference is TRUE LOVE. It's cute and a bit vague, but it is also sweet. It leaves room for almost any degree of affection.

While the world waits for TRUE LOVE to catch on, join me for a whirlwind tour of courtship alternatives to BOYFRIEND and GIRLFRIEND:

A BEAU, as the granddaughters of women born in the American South know, is a dream come true in Sunday suit and polished shoes. He is not (as I thought for years) so named because he favors bow ties, nor is he a bad speller (as I also thought): the word is French and means "beautiful" or "handsome." Beaus are given to *beaux gestes,* or gracious gestures (like bringing bouquets), a *beau ideal* is an idealized type, and Beaujolais, while having nothing directly to do with ideal lovers, is a great red wine.

A COHABITOR and a COMPANION can fill the bill, though the first suggests coexistence (and in the politics of love, détente is preferable) and the second is reminiscent of the shabbily genteel women of English novels, fourth daughters of impoverished vicars, earning their daily crust caring for wicked old (but rich) women who are murdered or deserve to be. The term CONSORT, on the other hand, packs a nice, built-in compliment: this is a royal spouse, or a person good enough to be one. It reeks, nevertheless, of presumption, and should be used only in private.

At first blush, FRIEND seems pretty weak stuff, but it can give off sparks when comparatively simple adjectives come into play. There's SPECIAL or BEST FRIEND, words that convey commitment without compulsion; from the 1930s through the 1950s, a GREAT AND GOOD FRIEND was the euphemistic code for mistress or lover, devised by journalists to sidestep libel laws. A GENTLEMAN FRIEND is an all-American synonym for BEAU (see above); a variation, GEN-

TLEMAN CALLER, typified the pathetic, pretentious fantasies of the southern mother in Tennessee Williams's *The Glass Menagerie.*

Like *FRIEND,* GIRL, GUY, and MAN seem pretty thin as love titles, but they take on considerable sensual and emotional weight with the addition of the possessive MY, especially in popular songs: the irreplaceable "My Best Girl's a Corker" was an 1890s hit, as was "My Girl Is a High Born Lady" by Barney Fagan, the Irishman who brought the cakewalk to America. French songwriter Maurice Yvain wrote "Mon Homme" in 1920 for Mistinguett (a café and concert singer who began life as Mademoiselle Bourgeoise but soon, under her stage name, became known for her long, lovely legs and a popular partnership with Maurice Chevalier). She took it to New York in 1924, where Fanny Brice sang it as "My Man" in the Ziegfeld Follies and, in 1928, gave the title to her first Hollywood movie. *Porgy and Bess* includes "My Man's Gone Now"; Carly Simon cut the album *Mind on My Man* in 1974. "He's My Guy" was a hit in 1943, and "My Best Girl" was a number in *Mame.* On the pop charts, Smokey Robinson seemed to corner the market in the 1960s with "My Guy" (sung by Mary Wells), "My Girl" (a number-one hit by the Temptations), and "My Girl Has Gone" (by the Miracles).

After all this possessiveness, it's surprising that WOMAN more often than not stands alone as a love title (although men sometimes add a "my" in social situations, as in "Bess,

You Is My Woman Now," another *Porgy and Bess* lyric). The direct address goes back generations: "Woman, Lovely Woman" was a hit in 1886. Bob Merrill wrote the lyrics to "You Are Woman" in *Funny Girl,* a musical based on the life of vaudeville star and actress Fanny Brice. Gary Puckett and the Union Gap had a hit in 1968 with "Woman Woman." The most memorable and most heartbreaking of all is John Lennon's 1981 "Woman," a tribute to his wife, Yoko Ono. It went to the top of the charts in 1981, a month after a crazy admirer shot him dead as he stood beside her.

HONEY is one of the edible endearments (see chapter 5) that can also announce an intimate relationship: "Russ is my honey." Another comestible defining term is SWEETIE; SWEETHEART will suffice too. However saccharine, these words have the advantage of being unisex, and both are infinitely preferable to saying "Russ is Sarah's LIVE-IN," an unfortunate label that makes a lover sound like household help, or maybe an indentured servant. A possibly more palatable alternative is MATE (also HOUSEMATE or ROOMMATE, with the sometimes bearable diminutive ROOMIE). It is vaguely unsettling, however, to learn that the writer Jack London called his wife MATE WOMAN.

Whether the party in question is a MAIN SQUEEZE, a MAIN ATTRACTION, or a MAIN EVENT, we get the message: this is somebody's central love interest, a term that presupposes "subordinate squeezes," "side shows," or "warm-up acts." A bloodless version of the same idea is SIGNIFICANT

OTHER, another unisex term that says the person so described is very important in a personal way but something "other" than a spouse.

A PARAMOUR, a basic love word explained in chapter 1, means "lover" and connotes a special or intense, heady passion—and I like it, although it may reveal too much for a casual introduction. But the American-style PARTNER, sometimes clarified with relentless, unromantic precision as LIFE PARTNER, goes too far the other way: it sounds like the insurance business to me, or a cattle roundup, or a precinct assignment.

PATOOTIE is a great word—silly, intimate, presumptuous, and funny. It's authentic American slang for BOYFRIEND or GIRLFRIEND, and doubles as slang for bottom or derrière. Often modified by SWEET, and good for either sex, it may be a derivation of sweet potato (the suggestion of Robert L. Chapman).

A POSSLQ (pronounced *possel-cue*) is the Census Bureau classification for Person of Opposite Sex Sharing Living Quarters. It is also the least-romantic love word in this book, so bereft of the voodoo that we all do so well that it positively bedews PARTNER, above, with the sweet perspiration of anticipatory excitement.

A SUITOR is a male lover, usually one who sues, as in petitions, for a woman's affection or "hand" in marriage. This is an old-fashioned term, useful when a man is himself old-fashioned or traditional, or when the young woman's father is. Out of the loop entirely are SWAINS, an old word for youthful and ardent males, sometimes of the more rustic or hopeless sort, who specialize in pining away and the doldrums.

In the twelfth century, Marie, the Countess of Champagne (and, not incidentally, the daughter of Eleanor of

NINE SYMBOLS OF LOVE

The Ring
The Circle pin
The Heart
XXXs and *OOOs*
Turtledove
Octopus (in Japan)
Diamond
Knots, especially love knots (two parallel strands knotted), and "that subtle knot, which makes us man" (John Donne, "The Ecstasy")

Aquitaine, a magnificent woman of formidable sexual attraction, action, and a lusty, indomitable spirit) invented the "Court of Love"—a kind of philosophic and social game that amused her courtiers by adjudicating assorted love suits. In Case Number 1174, reported in *Cleopatra's Nose* by Jerome Agel and Walter D. Glanze, the verdict read:

> We *declare and we hold as firmly established that love cannot exert its powers between two people who are married to each other. For lovers give each other everything freely, under no compulsion of necessity; married people are in duty bound.*

Be that as it may, for those lovers who remain devoted even after marriage, affectionate names for one another include many of the above, as well as the hopelessly homey HUBBY and WIFEY, MY BETTER HALF (a term used by men), MY BALL AND CHAIN, MY BRIDE, MY OLD MAN, and MY OLD LADY. The humor writer Dave Barry has coined a high-tech version, suitable to the computer age: SPOUSAL UNIT.

What about the modifiers, qualifiers, and quantifiers? What accounts for that initial attraction, that undeniable VAVAVAVOOM, that makes one person stand out across a crowded room? It might be innate, indefinable, a "certain something." Whatever it is, the person usually seems ADORABLE, one of many flattering words that spin off the verb *to adore.* It's overused and sounds pretty tame, but it's not: the original sense is religious, as in adoring one's God, and true adoration plays footsie with sacrilege. Still, one passion leads naturally to another, so long ago ADORE became part of the language of romantic love. So too did its definitive cousins: a man might WORSHIP THE GROUND SHE WALKS ON, and RESPECT, HONOR, or FEAR her in the temporal temple of the boudoir.

We adore the ones we love because they are BEAUTIFUL, or in slangier terms, A "REAL BEAUT," or in fusty Latinate language, PULCHRITUDINOUS. A term so current it may be passé by the time you finish this paragraph is BUFF, which does not mean to spit and polish, or do a manicure, but is 1990s college-student slang to describe an attractive person of either sex: "Ashley looks totally buff in that exercise outfit."

We know CUTE is a problem for men: call him SEXY, SUAVE, MACHO, MANLY, and ALLURING to his face; save CUTE for when you're telling your best friend (female) why he's so irresistible. Used for a woman, the slang diminutive CUTIE means a cheap or available girl, but its customary use today is usually more benign. A lover who is DREAMY—A REAL DREAMBOAT—is ideal; in the 1940s, college students pursued DREAM BAIT along with higher education.

A GOOD-LOOKING—or GOOD-LOOKIN'—guy or gal is just that, and a GORGEOUS person is SIMPLY FABULOUS— that is, of fabled figure and mien. GORGEOUS itself first appeared in Old French, meaning finely dressed or elegant, or arrayed in brilliant colors, or dazzling. Not so long ago, it was a female-only adjective, but in the 1950s a wrestler endowed with long blond hair and alarmingly defined muscles took the ring name of Gorgeous George. The rest is recent history: young women now use the adjective to describe attractive men. He might be GORGEOUS TO DIE FOR, or DROP-DEAD GORGEOUS, though more often a loved one is a KNOCKOUT or a STUNNER. A LOOKER is almost a STUNNER, the object of admiring stares (but a starer is just rubbernecking, an act without any sexual or social merit).

In the curiously oblique language of love, the mild-mannered, inexact SOME takes on special force, or at least suggests a significant quantity, especially to those rendered inarticulate: "She is SOME kind of wonderful," a love-struck young swain of the twentieth century might remark to a buddy. Or, "Boy, she is SOME KIND OF WOMAN!" A HANDSOME man (or guy) has been a good-looking, fine-figured male since the sixteenth century, and "Hello, handsome" is a loving greeting, preferably uttered in a low, throaty voice. This word was unisex even before our egalitarian age; a plain but pleasing-featured woman might also be called "handsome." On the other hand, so might an interesting chest of drawers, or a reward for a lost dog.

TOOTHSOME, however, is usually reserved for women. It's an old-fashioned compliment, and as a child I wondered if it was used in olden times to describe women who were attractive because, even though they lived in an age bereft of modern dental hygiene, they still had all their teeth. Or did it mean they were delicious-looking, the sort a man might want to sink his teeth into, like an éclair? The dictionary was heavy and distracting (there were all those *other* T words!), but it had the answer: TOOTHSOME means "pleasant to taste, savory, and palatable," and we've been adding it to the pile of modifiers we heap on loved ones (and our imaginary plates) since the mid-nineteenth century.

If some kinds of *some*-full words are to die for, others are already dead: both EYESOME, meaning a person so good-looking he or she fills the eye, and LEESOME, meaning pretty, are archaic—underused, unloved, unwanted as endearing modifiers.

Temperatures rise and fall in the fields of love: previously an exclusively sexual adjective in love talk, HOT is now synonymous for very attractive, stylish, even up-to-date among American teenagers—"That new haircut is very hot." COOL, bless its beatnik heart, remains au courant and desirable, one generation to the next. Denotatively it means "moderately cold," "losing excitement and ardor," and "indifferent." But in slang, since 1820, *cool* has also meant calm impudence. Among jazz players it meant good, *verrrry* good, beginning about 1945; a "cool" jazz singer is one with a throaty voice and delivery. Teenagers and beatniks made *cool* synonymous with self-control and unflappable self-confidence in the early 1950s. To be "cool as a virgin" typifies this kind of open-eyed calm, and the connection with sex, albeit a tenuous one, goes back to the "cool ladies" of the late seventeenth century, camp followers who, according to Eric Partridge's *A Dictionary of Slang,* as edited by Paul Beale, sold brandy to the troops.

One size does not fit all, fortunately. While current fashion dictates that those who are SVELTE, SLIM, and SLENDER are immediately adorable, the word ZAFTIG—adopted into English from German—remains one of the kindest love adjectives in the language. It means pleasingly plump, and almost always applies to women. In fact, a fulsome shape will often stir mind and vocabulary, as these words, drawn from Paul Hellweg's *The Odd Word,* suggest: BATHYKOLPIAN (deep-bosomed), BUSTLUCIOUS (having a shapely breast), CALLIPYGIAN (having a shapely derrière, or bottom), EVANCALOUS (being pleasant to embrace), or VENUST (being beautiful like Venus).

It is but a heartbeat to more sensual admiration. Explicitly sexy adjectives include: AMOROUS, BUILT, BURSTING, CURVACEOUS, DESIRABLE, DEWY, DOWNY, EROTIC, ETHEREAL, FETCHING, FIRM, FULL, HEATED, HOT, JIGGLY, JUICY, LASCIVIOUS, LIBIDINOUS, LUSTY, MISTY, MOIST, MUSKY, POUTY, PUCKERED, SENSUAL, SENSUOUS, SILKY, SLICK, SLURPY, SMOOTH, SPICY, STACKED, VOLUPTUOUS, and WET.

When we meet someone who can be described by one or more of the modifiers in this chapter, we know it because we ARE ATTRACTED, or perhaps our EYES LOCK. We may even experience TINGLING or TITILLATION, also known as EX-

CITEMENT and AROUSAL, or become aware of a pounding heart or roaring ears. The object of our instinctive, procreative energies is someone who can AMUSE, BEGUILE, CHARM, DAZZLE or BEDAZZLE, DELIGHT, ENTERTAIN, and SEND. Since the advent of the electrical age we may, when we encounter a REAL TURN-ON, feel lit up like a light bulb that suddenly gets a surge of hormonal juice. After awhile, we DATE, KEEP COMPANY, or GO OUT WITH, FIND or MAKE TIME FOR, and sometimes WITH, the OBJECT OF OUR AFFECTIONS.

HOT TALK

Where true Love burns, Desire is Love's pure flame;
It is the reflex of our earthly frame,
That takes its meaning from the nobler part,
And but translates the language of the heart.
—COLERIDGE, "DESIRE," 1830

"When You're Hot, You're Hot."
—JERRY REED, 1971

YES JUST HAPPENS to be one of the sexiest words in the language. If you don't believe me, go read the last sixty pages of James Joyce's *Ulysses,* which (if it's a library copy) will fall open naturally to that very section. This chapter is an exploration of sexually explicit love terms—grossly delicate, plainly tricky, unblushingly flushed. It is dedicated to Harriet Y., also known as Harriet Why Not. Harriet is a lawyer I know, a petite, very feminine woman who dresses demurely and has been married for decades to the same man, by whom she has children she dearly loves. But what impresses people when they first meet Harriet is her earthy, sensual appreciation of the world: she salts and peppers almost every utterance with sexual innuendo; she delights in all things—including the word "thing," for example—sexily suggestive. Shown a child's watch whose face featured a picture of a frog, she said that the second hand looked "like a little green penis, going round and round." Leaning back casually against her husband one evening, she interrupted herself to tell him not to move "because this position is good." She is outrageous, she makes me laugh. So this chapter is for Harriet, a woman who often leaves verbal decorum at the door.

Most sexy language is not socially de rigueur. It wouldn't be quoted in *The New York Times,* which primly excludes vulgarisms that we know to be BLUE, COMMON, CRUDE, LEWD, OFFENSIVE, RACY, RAUNCHY, TABOO, TASTELESS, and X-RATED (or, in the current terminology, NC-17-RATED). But since when is sex polite? It's a fact of lust that many people find pleasure in using coarse terms with lovers, those dear objects of our tender admiration.

The mixture of lewd and lovely may be a fact, but it remains curious. Why do we risk coming close to or skidding splat into crudity? Doesn't bad language degrade romance?

It depends.

Intimate, officially unacceptable sex talk can coexist with romance partly because, like love itself, it's dangerous, a verbal thrill. It approximates in words some of the improper, heedless frenzy that goes with arousal; it is itself a

TURN-ON, a COME-ON, SUGGESTIVE, even PROVOCATIVE. Sexy, so-called "bad" language defies rules of politeness and propriety (two qualities not often found keeping company with passion, anyway); raunchy talk makes its own rules, chooses its own vocabulary. A private, daring idiom can mark the boundaries of a private, personal world. Lovers are naked with one another, and they use words with one another that no one else will hear quite the same way because they have a special, intimate understanding. Hot talk, each utterance burning with the incandescent heat of desire, is the dialect for murmured lisps and whispers, for unguarded, essential truth, for those moments when—to use a current phrase for sex—they GET DOWN AND DIRTY.

An old song from the 1940s, "Speak Low," advises us to speak low when we speak love. (Music by Kurt Weill, lyrics by Ogden Nash in close collaborative embrace with Shakespeare, who, in *Much Ado About Nothing,* gives the following line to Don Pedro: "Speak low if you speak love," II, i, 104.) Whether you take that advice to mean soft and husky, or common and coarse, it's good counsel. Often, fine sexy talk of the soft and husky variety flirts, or experiments, with what is common and coarse.

No single chapter (or even two) can contain all the syllabic sizzle we speakers of English can roll through our imaginations and off our tongues, but it is possible to take its THROBBING, TREMBLING, perpetually ENGORGED pulse. As a favorite topic of conversation, sex has a perpetually expanding list of relevant nouns, adjectives, and (especially) verbs.

But *caveat amator:* going beyond polite does not mean going beyond respect or regard. In loving hot talk, as in all loving parlance, it is not so much what you say as how you say it.

PLAYGROUNDS

Just as stone phalluses marked the way to HOUSES OF PLEA-SURE or HOUSES OF PRIAPUS (the ancient god of gardens and male virility) in ancient Pompeii, so today classical terms and allusions mark the sites and sights of sexual play. Lovers PLEASURE one another still, the word PHALLIC describes *anything* (the Washington Monument, for example) that resembles a penis, and PRIAPIC continues to flesh out, as an adjective, someone or thing obsessed with male sexual power. Virgins, alleged or otherwise, can demand a high price for purchased sex in a HOUSE, also known as a CALL HOUSE, CAT HOUSE, HOUSE OF ILL REPUTE, JOY HOUSE, JUKE HOUSE, SPORTING HOUSE, STEW HOUSE, and WHORE HOUSE, BORDELLO and BROTHEL. In San Francisco at the turn of the century, the sex-for-sale business was located on a two-block street off Union Square ironically labeled MAIDEN LANE, now a posh shopping area. Such areas were called RED-LIGHT DISTRICTS, in recognition of the display that signaled an establishment was open for business.

When sex graduates into relationships, locales shift. For teenagers, it's the BACK SEAT OF A CHEVY (or whatever car they can get the keys to), a spare dorm bed, a friend's spare dorm bed. A man might finance a LOVE NEST, a PRIVATE HIDEAWAY, or a regular room in a favorite hotel. Women often retreat to their BOUDOIRS, home at last in a city apartment or a suburban split level.

PLAYERS

Sex seems to objectify individuals, to reduce them to their looks. Women get the most attention, but current idiom attempts some gender equity. A handsome man, for example, might HAVE BEDROOM EYES (Elvis Presley pretty much defined the look), or be REALLY RIPPED (that is, have rippling muscles) or HUNG (a reference to genital size). He might be an ADONIS, a SEX GOD, a STUD, or a STALLION. If he wants to be kept by a rich woman, he is a GIGOLO or, in the 1990s, a BOY TOY.

A woman can be HOT, a BABE, a PIECE, a RAGTIME GIRL (who could be anything from sweetheart to prostitute), a TOMATO, a SEDUCTRESS, a SEXPOT, or a SLUT (very popular among the preteen set). A FAST GIRL was once a LUSTY WENCH. If she is NOT A NICE GIRL (so our mothers told us), she may be NAUGHTY, a word that is a contraction of *ne* and *aught,* and used to mean *not worth anything* (just as our mothers told us).

If glimpsed on the arm of an aging politico, any of the above females may be a BIMBO, which is surprising: in 1900, that word meant "male thug," in 1920 "baby." Only in the late 1920s did it come to mean a sexually available young woman. The word is probably Italian in origin, from *bambino* (baby); it was also, writes Robert L. Chapman, a name for the monkey that went begging, cup in hand, for an Italian organ grinder.

A BIMBO may become a MISTRESS, a fascinating word. As a title, *mistress* comes from *mystery,* and before that the Latin word *magister,* meaning teacher or master. It's one more love term that has a split personality: in the Renaissance, a mistress was the feminine of master—one who had mastery over things because he knew its mysteries, or its secrets. A mistress ruled a man's heart, knew his secrets; the term was a compliment. By the seventeenth century, the shortened form of mistress was MRS., and over the next hundred years or so that word—in pronunciation a slurred *missus,* as soft as a growing waistline—became the essence of polite, middle-class female address. It was, in a word, ho-hum, exactly why a man might yearn for whatever he thought he meant by MISTRESS.

Which may explain why, in fact, the longer form put on her high-heel slippers and went dancing the light commitment: while Mrs. took root in middle-class morality, the meaning of MISTRESS evolved from true love to preferred sexual companion. As playwright William Wycherley wrote, "A mistress should be like a little country retreat near the town; not to dwell in constantly, but only for a night and away." The definition stuck: today a MISTRESS provides sexual congress, company, and sometimes conversation to a man on a regular basis. In return she sometimes gets cash, the comforts of home, and credit cards.

A KEPT WOMAN is a mistress whose arrangement definitely includes the upkeep, paid by a man not her husband (but, frequently, someone else's). She may be a LITTLE BIT OF STUFF he has ON THE SIDE. An outdated but more charming, frivolous synonym is LOOSE or LIGHT WOMEN; in the seventeenth and eighteenth centuries, POPLOLLIES were the granddaughters, etymologically and occupationally, of late sixteenth-century POPLETS. A considerably less delightful term is NECESSARIES, an eighteenth-century word for the women men slept with; it reminds me of PESSARIES, which have since the fifteenth century been vaginal suppositories. A 1925 euphemism for MISTRESS was HONEYSTAR, but it too has been abandoned for LOVER, or LIVE-IN, or— too often it seems—CODEPENDENT.

LOVE FOR SALE

Now, then, forever, and always: dozens of words and phrases in English identify those whose job it is to sell sex. They are PROSTITUTES, of course, and CALL GIRLS (on call through a service by telephone, they will visit a man, usually in a hotel room). A slew of women who work in THE WORLD'S OLDEST PROFESSION get their business on the streets: HOOKERS, LADIES OF THE NIGHT, STREETWALKERS, and WORKING GIRLS, to name a few. SCARLET WOMEN might be in THE PROFESSION, too, given to traipsing through streets lit by the aforementioned red lights, but in Western culture the association of the color scarlet with unsanctioned lust has more to do with a sensual style preference than professionalism. Chaucer's Wife of Bath, sexy as all get out but a legally wed wife five times over, wore scarlet stockings. Nathaniel Hawthorne splashed that shade of uncontrollable passion across the American consciousness in *The Scarlet Letter* in 1850.

The disparaging SLUT is a simplified form of the original word, SLUTTE (pronounced SLUT-ta), dating from the fifteenth century, and it too can mean prostitute. But it has more to do with messiness than morals: first and foremost, a slut is a slovenly woman, a slattern, untidy, unclean—in short, not a home ec major. A slut's most frequent adjectival companion: foul. She could also be a kitchen maid, or a mischievous and impudent girl; in *Joseph Andrews,* eighteenth-century novelist Henry Fielding writes, "I never knew any of these forward sluts to come to good," and a hundred years later Charles Dickens wrote of "a slut, a hussy." Yet there is a curious ambivalence that creeps in and around the edges of this word: *The Oxford English Dictionary* sets aside a short paragraph for its "playful" use, and for proof quotes from

Samuel Pepys's diary: "Our little girl Susan is a most ad-
mirable slut, and pleases us mightily."

What strikes me as quite remarkable in all this is the
very fine, frequently indistinguishable line drawn, for
women, between impudence and unworthiness. When I was
growing up, there was an old warning that schoolgirls half
believed: Don't chew gum, because girls who chew gum
will do *other* things—among them, wear patent-leather
shoes! (And everybody knew that girls who wore patent-
leather shoes were inviting boys to sneak peeks at their un-
derpants—reflected, of course, on the tops of those shiny
patent-leather shoes.) Girls who did so would soon GET
INTO TROUBLE and grow up to be LOOSE WOMEN.

A STRUMPET is beyond redemption, gloriously so. This is
a bald, unequivocally bad word for a bad woman, "a de-
bauched or unchaste woman, a harlot, prostitute." Ribald,
earthy, unashamed, unabashed, probably incapable of blush-
ing, she is an expert on the facts of life. She may be called
vile, common, and *abominable,* but *proud* and *grand* are not too
far-fetched. A 1545 writer noted, "They knowe the open
whoredome of the Babylonicall strompet."

The stalwart term WHORES, hale and hearty for over five
hundred years, still echoes through the streets, complete or
in its abbreviated form, HO. As with a lot of vulgar words,
the slur that goes with WHORE has eased somewhat in re-
cent years; it still means someone who does IT for money,
but the doer can be male or female, and the IT can be any-

thing—the creation of Madison Avenue ad copy, the construction of sculpture for a hotel lobby, the unloading of municipal bonds on old ladies—that produces quick profit for people who are capable of finer things.

Some eighteenth-century English synonyms for WHORE are still used, though not often—LADY OF PLEASURE, HARLOT—and in a way they are sexier than more modern, explicit terms because they carry with them the aura of a time when sin really was sinful. Other terms, more lusty and appealing, have gone the way of all flesh: BLOWSABELLES, DOXIES, LADY BIRDS, NYMPHS OF DELIGHT, and the inspiring, enthusiastic TICKLE TAIL FUNCTIONS.

CLASS TELLS

If WHORES today sell out in a variety of ways, COURTESANS—the high-priced professionals of antiquity—did too, but they set a certain standard. Aspasia, companion of the Athenian leader Pericles around 440 B.C., was literate and beautiful; the Greek word for her role is *hetaera,* and their home was a focus of Athenian culture, which suggests, to modern ears, something like the Parisian salons of the nineteenth century. One of the few Greek women whose histories were recorded, Aspasia reportedly advised Pericles on his decisions and speeches, and so may have influenced his drive toward greater democracy; his enemies accused her of improperly urging policies leading to the Peloponnesian

War, in which Athens ultimately failed. To get at Pericles, some accused Aspasia of "impiety," and she was condemned to death. But her lover pled so magnificently for her life that she was saved. In Renaissance Venice, COURTESANS moved freely in a society dedicated to commercial dominance and political intrigue. They were flamboyant, unashamed, and educated. As a sign of their licentious calling, they were traditionally "Titian-haired," sporting elaborate, flaming red coiffures the color of the pigment made famous by their local famous artist.

The root of the word COURTESAN is Latin: COHORS, meaning a troop or throng. The Italian word *corte* (court) comes from it, and the connection makes sense: unless they inherit the job, kings became kings by killing as many people as possible, an enterprise that required an army; their thronging advisors, the comrades who surrounded them in battle, made up their "court" in peacetime. These political and princely insiders became known, in time and in Italy, as *cortigianos* (male courtiers) and *cortigianas* (female courtiers) —the courtly cohort. The word became *courtisanes* in Old French, and *courtesans* in Renaissance England; in early days it applied to members of either sex skilled in courtly diplomacy. Their art had something to do with the medieval concept of courtesy, something to do with our modern understanding of courtship, but among royals in high places it was always thoroughly enmeshed in conspiracy, plots, fashion, indirection—and delivered in a language that almost qualified as a separate dialect. As an Englishman wrote of the Italian court in 1603, "To be discerned from the vulgar, they all in generall speak the courtesan."

But for all their skills and courtesies, and however wise their counsel, the women of the court were invariably, predictably objects of sexual speculation as well—and vulnerable (as powerful women are still) to a peculiarly debasing sort of smarmy innuendo. Inevitably, verbal refinements came into play: men of the court, statesmen and scoundrels alike, were *courtiers,* and women who sought political influence of their own were *courtesans,* offering sexual availability as part of the package. (The "nice" women at court might be among the queen's ladies-in-waiting, but only if the queen herself was chaste, or perceived to be so.)

The situation of a courtesan was precarious, but still, the term implied a certain cachet: "Your whore is for every rascall, but your Curtizan is for your Courtier," a writer noted in 1607. They could be "lewd" in Smollett's *Roderick Random* (1748), but the acceptance by Queen Alexandra of King Edward VII's courtesan-style mistresses, some of whom she invited to the dying king's bedside for fond farewells, was more in keeping with the quasi-honorable role they have played in history. Among Edward VII's great and good women friends: Lillie Langtry, Alice Keppel, and Jennie Churchill, Sir Winston Churchill's mother. Ralph C. Martin, Lady Churchill's biographer, describes her relationship to the king in a passage that neatly sums up the art and service of the courtesan:

> *She had a significant and lasting influence on him because he respected her judgment. He also knew he could rely on her. If he wanted a small private party arranged, he often asked her to oversee the compiling of the guest list and decide on the menu. Jennie knew his particular friends as well as his favorite foods. She knew what kind of music he liked. She knew the level of his impatience and boredom, the danger point of his anger, and what to do about them. In return, he was lavish in his gifts and in his open affection for her.*

Most of us do not mix love affairs and affairs of state: highly formal, political, and sexual alliances are, especially in still-Puritanical America, pretty rare stuff. Yet all of us can identify with these high-class lovers in one respect—language: hot talk bridges the social gap with delectable, daring sizzle, and social position is not the position that matters when lovers get physical. Powerful or otherwise, men and women seem to prefer, for passion, a vocabulary familiar (in both senses of that word), often low, frequently vulgar. Thus a modern prince reportedly told his mistress, in 1993, that he'd like to come back in his next life as her trousers. And when Edward VII remonstrated with his mistress Lillie Langtry that he'd spent enough money on her to buy a battleship, she retorted that he'd SPENT enough *"in her"* to float one.

Like all things human, the language of lust-filled love is subject to whim and fashion, and what we say we do when we enjoy one another sexually has a lot to do with when we say it—not just the hour of the day, though that counts too,

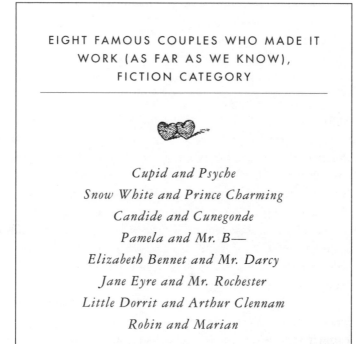

EIGHT FAMOUS COUPLES WHO MADE IT
WORK (AS FAR AS WE KNOW),
FICTION CATEGORY

Cupid and Psyche
Snow White and Prince Charming
Candide and Cunegonde
Pamela and Mr. B—
Elizabeth Bennet and Mr. Darcy
Jane Eyre and Mr. Rochester
Little Dorrit and Arthur Clennam
Robin and Marian

but the decade. In *Where Echoes Live,* a 1991 mystery novel by Marcia Muller, two characters run through a generational glossary of sex words. The speakers: Sharon McCone, Muller's middle-aged detective, and Rae, her young assistant, who says that she and her boyfriend Willie (whose name, by the way, is British slang for penis) spent much of the weekend "doing the wild thing."

> *". . . The what?*
> *"Wild thing. You know."*
> *"You mean . . ."*
> *"Yeah, that." She frowned, . . . "Well, what do you call it?"*
> *"Making love."*
> *"No, I mean informally. What does your generation call it?" . . .*
> *"Well, when I was in high school, we just said 'doing it' at first. But that was in the sixties and everybody wanted to be shocking, so before long it was 'fucking.'. . . And in the eighties we 'significantly related' or some such godawful phrase. And now . . . In my older brothers' day, I think they said 'going all the way.' My parents called it 'taking a nap' and sent us all to my aunt's house."*
> *"When I was in school, it was 'getting it on.' The grandmother who raised me called it 'having carnal knowledge' and forbade it."*

"What a long way we've come—doing the wild thing.
Can you also call it wild thinging?. . ."

MAKING LOVE. HAVING CARNAL KNOWLEDGE. DOING
IT. HAVING SEX. GOING ALL THE WAY. SIGNIFICANTLY RE-
LATING. FUCKING. TAKING A NAP. WILD THINGING. They
all mean sexual intercourse, and they all are terms that, be-
tween intimates, can be love talk.

In fact, Sharon and Rae barely scratch the surface. Other
synonyms for the sex act include: BALL, BANG, BED, BELLY,
BLOW, BOB, BOFF, BOINK, BONK, BOOGIE, (DO THE)
BOUNCY BOUNCY, BUFF, CAT AROUND, DICK, DO, DO IT,
(HAVE A) FLESH SESSION, FROLIC, GET DOWN, GET HORI-
ZONTAL, GET IT ON, GET LAID, GET (or HAVE) YOUR ASHES
HAULED, GO BOOM BOOM (also toddler slang for *fall down*),
GO TO BED WITH, HAVE, HAVE AT IT, HUMP, JUMP YOUR
BONES (a favorite of detective novelist Robert Parker's so-
phisticated lovers Spenser and Susan Silverman), MAKE,
MAKE WHOOPEE, MESS AROUND, PERFORM, PLEASURE,
POKE (American wrangler slang, used throughout Larry
McMurtry's *Lonesome Dove*), PORK, PUT OUT, ROGER (espe-
cially in Britain, best on video when uttered by Sir John
Gielgud), SCREW, SLEEP WITH (the curious euphemism em-
ployed to mystify small children), SOW WILD OATS, and
SPORT. In the 1992 movie *A League of Their Own,* a talent
scout refers to sex as a PICKLE TICKLE; Chaucer used the
verb SWIVE.

Does anyone MAKE LOVE anymore? Yes, but we may choose to say instead that we GO ROUND THE WORLD, PLAY HIDE THE SALAMI, HAVE A ONE-NIGHT STAND or a QUICKIE (or a NOONER, a MATINEE, or a LUNCH TREAT). Part of the experience may include COPPING A FEEL, DIDDLING, FEELING UP, or asking, "MAY I GO UP YOUR SHIRT?" (established etiquette at high school dances, circa 1990). A good but forgotten word for it is GRUBBLE, which is *not* what a lecherous turkey does but in the seventeenth century was a synonym, more or less, for FONDLE. In John Dryden's translation of Ovid's *Amores,* judged obscene at the time, the poet advises his lover to find him in a crowd ". . . and there we cannot miss, /Perhaps to grubble, or at least to kiss."

And then there's FUCK, too important for a mere cameo appearance in a list. One of the hardiest of all English words, it dates in its present form to about 1200. Chaucer used it. So did Henry Miller, James Joyce, and almost every other "serious" twentieth-century American novelist. So do most teenage kids in America today. So does *Vanity Fair* (but not *The New York Times Magazine* or *Newsweek*). So, quite often, do lovers.

The trouble with this four-letter word in a book about love language is that it's *vulgar,* an adjective and concept so central to this chapter that it's worth its own paragraph. Defined as "common," *vulgar* comes from the Latin word *vulgus,* meaning the mob or the common people—so far, nicely democratic. But *vulgar* splashes the distinct stains and aromas of barnyard reality across any noun it modifies. Secondary meanings include "a lacking in cultivation, perception, or taste: COARSE; morally crude, undeveloped or unregenerate: GROSS; ostentatious or excessive in expenditure or display: PRETENTIOUS; offensive in language: EARTHY; lewd or profanely indecent: OBSCENE."

And FUCK is the perfect example of vulgarity: a democratic word used by members of all classes; coarse, gross, sometimes pretentious, always earthy, usually obscene. It crops up, in a manner of speaking, in dozens of explicit, crude, unloving expressions.

To wit (though wit is not always employed with this overused word): FUCK YOU, FUCKED OVER, FUCKED UP. A FUCKER is a loathsome ne'er-do-well, feeling FUCKED OUT is being really, really tired, and FUCKING AROUND is goofing off. There's even FUCKING WELL, which, after all the negatives, carries an emphatically positive charge, as in "Your analysis of the First Amendment was fucking well done, Lloyd."

There are plenty of so-called "polite" stand-ins for this stand-up word: Chaucer's Wife of Bath uses FUTTER; we also have FORNICATE, FUG, FUGGER, FRIG (usually used in an adjective form, as in THIS FRIGGIN' COLD WEATHER), and TO DO A FLUTTER (a really lovely descriptive euphemism since about 1875). The early nineteenth-century term HONEYFUGGLE meant to cheat, swindle, or to make romantic sexual love. The code phrase in the first grade is THE

F-WORD. A euphemism from baby talk for those who are irredeemably squeamish is FIDDLESTICKS.

Where does all this lead? The literal answer is easy: to have an orgasm is TO BLOW YOUR TOP, CLIMAX, COME, and GET OFF. In Shakespeare's time the verb was TO SPEND, and the word, if not the event, has had some lasting power.

YOU'VE GOT THAT METAPHORIC FEELING

Sexual synonyms are almost always some kind of metaphor, implicit or otherwise. Consider HORNY, a term that dates from ancient times and, until recently, was an exclusively male index of arousal. In literature and gesture, horns symbolize a cuckold, a man whose wife is unfaithful and who presumably finds himself in a state of unrelieved, hornlike tumescence since she does her cavorting elsewhere. Pan—in language the Greek word for *all,* in mythology the wondrous, shocking creature literally divided between his human self and his goat self—is sexually avid, smelly, hoofed, with horns on his head and copulation on what passes for his mind. He's the god of herds and pastures; he's sylvan, he's sensual, he's got IT. When Christians made pagan rites passé, they had to redefine the ubiquitous, licentious Pan; he became a manifestation of the devil, called in Scotland AULD HORNY.

In some circles, such as those frequented by novelist

Kingsley Amis, HORN is slang for penis—especially if a lusty young man sees a pretty PIECE walk by and suffers or enjoys the physical consequences. Yet, though a man may be reminded of an animal's horn by his stiffened body part, though he may fantasize himself a stag in rut, vital spirits coursing up hills and down curving rills—still, the part in question does not magically become a horn but is only *like* a horn, and that's what poets and English teachers call metaphoric language.

Lovers may feel an ITCH—a real sexual tickle or a general need like the SEVEN-YEAR ITCH, allegedly experienced by husbands after seven years of marriage to the same woman and studied in depth in the movie starring Marilyn Monroe. For metaphor techies, this is synecdoche, citing a part for the whole or the whole for a part, and it's been going on for- ever. A woman is a *skirt* in (only slightly) passé American slang, and Shakespeare used *sweet blowse* in *Titus Andronicus* for what Dr. Johnson glossed, in the eighteenth century, as "a ruddy, fat-faced wench."

Men allude to their own needs and arousal as having HOT ROCKS, a HARD ON, or needing to GET SOME, a term and condition so common that it makes up the frequent male- to-male greeting, "Hiya Sam, gettin' any?" Men may de- scribe their erections as BONERS, their huge erections as BLUE STEELERS (but a STEELY DAN is a dildo). They may also FEEL HAIRY, or FEEL STROKED. Both sexes can be HOT TO TROT.

The Great American Metaphor for sex is TO SCORE, and when that happens it's because a lover COVERS THE BASES in the Great American Game: FIRST BASE (kissing), SECOND BASE (touching above the waist), THIRD BASE (touching below the waist), and HOME (intercourse). Obviously, if the seduction attempt fails, the lover STRIKES OUT. Getting HOME is also known as GOING ALL THE WAY; in the 1930s TO MAKE OUT meant to have sex, but nowadays it just means kissing and caressing, also known as PETTING.

The language for oral sex is almost ecstatically metaphoric: TO HOOVER (a reference to the vacuum cleaner), TO DO A HUM JOB, TO BE A PETER EATER, TO BE A FLUTE or PICCOLO PLAYER, TO PUT LIPSTICK ON HIS DIPSTICK, TO GIVE or SERVE HEAD, and TO PLAY TONSIL HOCKEY. The slang word GAM usually means *leg*, as in "that woman has gorgeous gams." However, in one of the funniest citations by Paul Beale in the 1984 edition of *A Dictionary of Slang*, a Malaysian prostitute in 1954 explained her reluctance to service some men in a bar by saying: "I no fuck. I holiday. But, I give you gam for ten bucks." Perhaps the connection is by way of the THIRD LEG, below.

E R O G E N O U S   Z O N E S

Sit down, clear your mind, and remember that judgment is essential when attempting the spit-slicked slopes of affectionate hot talk. Some terms for body parts—PRICK, for example, also meaning an abusive, infuriating, and objectionable male—are only derogatory. The same goes for the multiplicity of coarse terms used for female genitalia in a degrading or demeaning way. Some examples: GASH, NOTCH, SLIT, and TWAT.

An almost always coarse and insulting word about women is CUNT, meaning vulva. Its origins are ancient: from what *Webster's Ninth New Collegiate Dictionary* calls New Latin (*cunnus,* meaning "vulva," also one of the root words in the technical sexual term CUNNILINGUS), to Middle English *cunte,* by way of Middle Low German *kunte* (meaning "female pudenda") and related etymologically to Middle High German *kotze* ("prostitute"). It also connects to the Old English word *cwithe,* which means "the womb."

We owe much of what we know about this word to Eric Partridge's late 1930s edition of *A Dictionary of Slang;* so opprobrious is the term that it was excluded from *The Oxford English Dictionary* in 1932 and *The Shorter Oxford Dictionary* in 1933. The 1963 Signet edition of *Hamlet* suggests, with a faint-hearted evasiveness that surrounds scholarly discussion of this word, that the prince's lewd references to COUNTRY MATTERS with Ophelia is "a pun on the vulgar word for pudendum."

Just how bad is this bad word? In the beginning, CUNT was a common, but not obscene noun, sounding a lot like another common Middle English word for female genitalia, *quyente* (itself probably a combination of the Old French *coing* and the Old English *kunte*). CUNT wasn't the kind of word a courtier might proclaim loudly in the upper levels of society, but Chaucer (a statesman and courtier in real life) did come close in *The Canterbury Tales:* The Wife of Bath, no shy wallflower, refers to her QUEINTE. (She also calls it her BELE CHOSE, medieval French for "fair thing" and her QUONIAM, which I roughly translate into late twentieth-century English as "whatever.")

However, reversing the usual trend of sex words, CUNT grew more insulting and ugly over time. It has been considered unprintable since the 1700s. In the early seventeenth century, John Fletcher—whom Paul Beale characterizes as "no prude"—referred to it in this roundabout way: "They write *sunt* with a C, which is abominable." In 1759, Voltaire used it obliquely in *Candide,* giving the name Cunegonde to his naïve hero's sweetheart, a fetching creature who loses all of her innocence, half her posterior, but none of her heart. By the twentieth century, CUNT was the most taboo word around, a very derogatory term for women (and sometimes men).

In 1928, D. H. Lawrence began trying to get *Lady Chatterley's Lover* in print—a long battle, it turned out, because the book was banned in the United States until 1959 and Britain until 1960. In telling the story of a passionate, explicitly sexual affair between an upper-class Englishwoman and a lower-class gamekeeper who worked on her husband's estate, Lawrence dared to use CUNT—the word itself, spelled out, without ellipsis, coy rhyme, etymological allusions or indirection. The gamekeeper, Mellors, having just made love to Lady Constance Chatterley, tells her:

> *Let me be. I like thee. I luv thee when tha lies theer. A woman's a lovely thing when 'er's deep ter fuck, and cunt's good. Ah luv thee, thy legs, an' th' shape on thee, an' th' womanness on thee. Ah luv th' womanness on thee. Ah luv thee wi' my ba's an' wi' my heart.*

It's a shocker, all right: Lawrence uses taboo language without taboo intent. His comments might not please every lover, but there is nothing insulting about the use of the four-letter words in this passage: they are part of his natural working vocabulary. The lady, and she is a Lady, takes no offense, and this is exactly how love can launder usually offensive language.

As always, the greater the obsession, the more words there are to describe it. The terms our society recognizes for female breasts include BALLOONS, BAZOOMS, BAZOONGIES, BIG BROWN EYES, BOOBS, BOOSIASMS, CHICHIS, DUGS, GARBANZOS, KNOCKERS, HOOTERS, PAPS, POTATOES, TATAS, TITS, TITTIES. Today a BUBBIE is usually short for BUBBELEH, a Yiddish term of endearment meaning *sweetie pie;* in 1703, however, BUBBIES was an affectionate term for a woman's breasts.

Euphemisms for the vagina and female genitalia are numerous, not surprising since according to one study men think of sex every nineteen seconds. Shaw's term was HER SEX, a modest phrase surprisingly employed today by the very explicit American novelist Anne Rice, who, at one point early on in her career, devoted herself to hard- and soft-core pornography. Other phrases, gathered from books of slang, euphemisms, and risqué novels, include: BEARDED CLAM, BEAVER, BOX, BUSH, CLIT, CLITTY, COOCH, CRACK OF HEAVEN, FUN PIE, GARDEN OF EDEN, HONEY POT, LAP (from *Romeo and Juliet,* where the hero talks of a young woman's being willing or not willing to "ope her lap"), MOUNT OF VENUS or VENUS MOUNT (a bit of classical imagery still readily understood today), NOOKY, PIECE (as in "piece of that," or "piece of ass"), POGIE, PRIVATES, PUSSY, TAIL, and the completely unromantic TOOL SHED.

Like HORNY, the basic imagery is ancient. In *The Perfumed Garden,* a love manual by the Tunisian Shayleh Umar ibn Muhammed al-Nefzawi and written about 1500, similar synonyms are recorded meaning SLIT, CRUSHER, BOTTOM-LESS, and THE DELICIOUS. In the 1500s, Queen Elizabeth I of England once chided her advisors, "Had I been born crested and not cloven, ye would not treat me thus."

Flower imagery is also common. In 1941, Orson Welles and Herman Mankiewicz made *Citizen Kane,* a celluloid character study based on William Randolph Hearst's life; as a remarkable "inside" joke, they made the word ROSEBUD the film's mysterious symbol, which they explained at the end as the name of the sled that Kane had—and lost—as a little boy. But according to Jerome Agel and Walter D. Glanze, authors of *Cleopatra's Nose,* a book on popular phrases, there was more to it: the filmmakers knew it was Hearst's private name for the genitalia of his mistress, one-time starlet Marion Davies.

Words for the penis abound: BALDHEADED HERMIT, BIG ONE, BONER, COCK, CROTCH COBRA, DING DONG, DINGLE DANGLE, DINGUS, DIPSTICK, DONG (as in LONG DONG SILVER, star of pornographic screen and, in October 1991, the Senate Judiciary Hearings on the confirmation of Supreme Court Justice Clarence Thomas), DOODLE, DORK (which has evolved since the 1980s into a milder-meaning equivalent to JERK), ELEVENTH FINGER, GHERKIN (because it rhymes with JERKIN', of course), HAMMER, HOSE, JOYSTICK, LOVE MUSCLE, MAYPOLE, PECKER, POKER, RAMROD, ROD, SAUSAGE, SHLONG (from the Yiddish word for snake), SHORT ARM, STIFFY, THING, THIRD ARM, THIRD LEG, TOOL, the wonderfully suggestive TROUSER TROUT and the appalling TUBE STEAK, TWANGER, WAZOO, WHANG, WINKIE (but surely never WEE WILLY WINKIE), WOODY, and YING-YANG. Supermodel Cindy Crawford once dismissed rumors that she was gay thus: "For me, though, it's like Sharon Stone has said, 'It don't mean a thing, if it ain't got that SCHWING!' "—a super show business one-liner in which the 1990s comic Mike Myers's preferred penis synonym collides with Duke Ellington's 1932 hit song title.

There also is a curious assortment of "given name" euphemisms, as if this part of man is a separate being altogether: a short list includes DICK, JOHNNIE, JOHN THOMAS (from Lawrence in *Lady Chatterley's Lover*), LONG JOHN, MR. HAPPY, PETER, and ROGER. Frau Goethe referred to her husband's penis as HERR SCHONFUSS, "Mr. Sweet Foot."

A friend of a friend, whose husband's penis is bent, calls him CAP'T, short (if that is the right word) for Captain Hook. The aforementioned WILLY is British slang, reportedly the reason why the present Prince William of England is called "Wills" as a nickname and the source of much adult—well, allegedly adult—giggling in the 1993 Disney movie about a trapped whale, *Free Willy.* Following the summer crime sensation of 1993, when Lorena Bobbitt, resident of a state that boasts "Virginia Is for Lovers," cut off the penis of John Wayne Bobbitt in a conjugal quarrel, *The Washington Post* referred to the parted part as: WALLY, ALISTAIR, KING GUSTAV V, and MR. BELVEDERE. *Newsweek,* which reported the euphemisms, also noted a headline in *The Ottawa Citizen:* "Sad Saga of a Wife's Attempt to Free Willy."

As with vagina, so with penis: much of this male imagery is familiar, old news continually reinvented. Arabic equivalents translate as CROWBAR, ONE-EYED BALD ONE, THE RUMMAGER, and THE RANSACKER. Not all of these ancient penis "euphemisms," if they can be called that, suggest violence; in *The Secrets of the Jade Chamber,* a book of sexual advice and technique written in China around the second century A.D., the penis was called the JADE PEACH (and the vagina, the JADE GATE).

There's more. What medical books call testicles, conversationalists of various classes and backgrounds call BALLS, COJONES, CRYSTALS, DOODADS, DOHICKIES, EQUIPMENT, FAMILY JEWELS, NECESSARIES, NUGGETS (alternatively, LOVE NUGGETS), NUTS, ROCKS, STONES, and TOOL BAG.

For semen: CREAM, CUM, JELLY, JUICE, and JISM. In an extraordinary scene in William Styron's novel *Sophie's Choice,* the exquisite heroine uses some as a face cream.

For the hips and buttocks of either sex: ASS, BOODY, BUNS, BUTT, CAN, TOOKIS (Yiddish)—although BUTT and the Yiddish variants are often used without any sexual intent as synonyms for BOTTOM (itself a euphemism for the rather ungentle sound of *buttocks*).

NOUNS YOU CAN'T TRUST

Nouns that define or identify a man who is sexually eager or especially focused on seduction include CASANOVA (a real person who lived and recounted his amours in the eighteenth century), DON JUAN, LIBERTINE, LOTHARIO, MAN ABOUT TOWN, PROFLIGATE, RAKE, SEDUCER, SENSUALIST, TRAVELING MAN, VOLUPTUARY, WOLF, or WOMANIZER.

Fast women often have a bad rep and are known as FEMMES FATALES, FLOOZIES, GOLD BRICKERS, LADY PIRA-

NHAS, MARRIAGE WRECKERS, MAN EATERS, and MAN STEALERS. Also suspect are GROUPIES and STAR FUCKERS (girls who prefer sex partners who excel at pop music, sports, or politics), JEZEBELS, LOLITAS, the too familiar SLUTS, and TRAMPS. A HUSSY might be a tramp, but she might also just be a tad stuck-up, American southern-style. Women who are willing are EASY, EASY LAYS, FAST, LOOSE, PUSHOVERS (circa the 1940s to the present), or have ROUND HEELS.

A VAMP is a ruthless female bent on a man's destruction, one who seems to suck the soul right out of an infatuated victim. Or she can be a more or less charming FLIRT and COQUETTE. Either way she is very sexy—hence attractive and enticing despite her pitiless outlook on life and love. VAMP is also a verb: a woman can VAMP a man by parading her seductive ways before him.

A male or female who FOOLS AROUND too much may become BAD NEWS, a DEBAUCHEE, a DEGENERATE, a DIRTY OLD MAN or WOMAN, or REAL TROUBLE. A noun that has disappeared, and good riddance, is SMELLSMOCK, which in the sixteenth and seventeenth centuries meant a licentious man. It hardly bears thinking about, but the term seems to derive from the odoriferous aura that surrounded a certain priest who did not keep his vow of celibacy. From the same era comes the still ubiquitous ADULTERER and the outdated BEDSWERVER, or CUCKOLDER.

I've always been troubled by the apparent connection between ADULT and ADULTERY: is it so inevitable that men and women will cheat on each other that the words stem from the same root? No. ADULT comes from the Latin word *adultus,* past participle of the verb *adolescere,* meaning to grow up. ADULTERY comes from the Latin word *adulterium,* which means adultery, and though not directly related it is very similar to the Latin verb *adultarare,* to pollute.

That said, bawdy behavior and language does have its place among adults. It can even be sweet. For a poignant and classy example of low language that moves hearts, here are two lines from "John Kinsella's Lament for Mrs. Mary Moore," by William Butler Yeats:

> *What shall I do for pretty girls*
> *Now my old bawd is dead?*

CHAPTER 4

BABY LOVE, MY BABY LOVE TALK

*L*OVE WORDS HAVE TO START somewhere, somehow, even if no one, not even songwriter Lorenz Hart, "knows where or when." But we can guess.

Picture a baby's crib. Add a doting mother and father, grandparents, aunts and uncles, even a bighearted big sister or brother—all peering over the sides at an unimaginably tiny little package of sleeping infant humanity. They are all holding their breaths and then—

Look! Shhh! So little! What a beautiful baby!

Verbal schmoozing begins the moment we are swaddled, coddled, cuddled, and cradled in the first sensations of caring tenderness. It's a time of essential acceptance and approval; we start then a long affair of feeling and family, a passion woven of idealistic expectation and qualifying reality. First-love utterances are, very often, MAMA and DADA, two key words in baby talk, the speech parents teach.

How appealing this is, how soothing! How thrilling and

restful at the same time, especially later, when grown-up babies have power, but also schedules and responsibilities. Giving and receiving love are splendid feelings, a blessed relief, an endorsement: it makes us feel good inside our skins. When obligation hums its distracting tune, when the facts of life dog our heels and nip at our calves—at those all too frequent moments unconditional love is what we crave.

So, in the privacy of my home, when I shut the door on implacable demand and intractable reality, I am fluent in two distinct dialects of baby talk—one for babies and one for My Baby. Spelled out, on paper, the languages look almost identical, but context makes all the difference: who speaks to whom, and how, and when. We call our children HONEY, ANGEL, and SWEETIE, and make dinner; we call our lovers HONEY, ANGEL, and MY SWEET, and make love.

If you think about it, and I have, the inclination to mix up baby talk and grown-up love talk is not a little strange. Sure, it's cute. Who among us has not invented anew what poets four hundred years ago called LOOKING BABIES IN THE EYES? That's the reflection of oneself in a lover's eyes—the tiny little mirrored image, a big person made cute and small, the self projected on a screen that is literally of the loved one's making and close enough to kiss. To post-Freudian thinkers, this might symbolize the narcissism of love; to Renaissance image makers, it was a picture of the infant god Cupid, the mythological embodiment of love. Farfetched? Who cares?

Our less subtle age may color the meanings more boldly, but the basic references hold fast:

> *"C'mon,* BABY, let's dance!"
> "BABY, you look great!"
> "Whatta BABE!!"

Those who don't qualify in the BABE stakes are usually WANNABE BABES, whether they admit it or not. As the Big Bopper himself, one J. C. Richardson, groaned in anguished delight: "KISS me, BAAA-BEH. Ohhhhh, you *know* what I like!"

But I have to ask: does BABY (or BAAA-BEH) talk hopelessly jumble innocents and adventurers? Does it blur the line between real little kids and adults—a dangerous game for children? Does it infantilize grown-up lovers, providing the verbal means to sidestep maturity and equality in love relationships, where it is usually women, not men, who are the "babies"?

Of course it does. Sometimes. Yet within reason, if adults remember they are playing, baby love talk is what it's supposed to be: harmless, delightful, restorative, tolerant. To BABY means to indulge, to dote on, to humor, to wait on—in short, to love, and usually to love adults who are not normally "babied." When lovers relapse into childish affectations it's because they hope the ersatz infantilisms will somehow reinvent and reinforce the long-gone, unconditional love of once upon a time. It's a test: if you really love me, you will tolerate me when I feel childish. You will adore me, you will want to understand me, you will wait breathlessly for my every utterance, and *you will like it excessively.* In short, you will give me an A+ in acceptance, and A is for Always.

What is this thing called baby talk? The speech of very young children is a special, ostensibly simplified (but in fact complicated) variant of adult language taught by adults in one-on-one tutorials. In *Word Play: What Happens When People Talk,* Peter Farb found it in languages as diverse as Latin and Native American Comanche. It characteristically has a simple vocabulary and relies on extra-careful pronunciation—a deliberate, stretched-out enunciation that lends itself to singsong delivery. Nonsense rhymes abound, and simple sounds; when children are newborn, we say BAY-BEE to them (or MAKE GOO-GOO EYES over them). We make a sound written as KITCHY KITCHY KOO, sure to grab a baby's attention with the clicky K sounds followed by the soothing KOO syllable.

When adults talk to babies, redundancy is in: somehow it is more fun to say CHINNY CHIN CHIN than *chin.* Food is not food but a simple rhyme of pleasure: to wit, NUM NUMS, YUM YUMS, or YUMMIES. A toddler's verbal world is a bloodless Serengeti Plain of animal analogies, furry creatures, and bemusing non sequiturs: Are you my FUNNY BUNNY? My SILLY BILLY (GOAT)? My HAIRY CATERPILLAR? My TIGER

CUB? Diminutives—words that end in -a, -y, -ie, -ty, -tie, -ette, -kin, -kins, and -ling—crowd the linguistic water-holes of names and nicknames. A baby is not just SWEET and SWEETHEART, but a SWEETIE, a SWEETIE PIE, SWEET STUFF, SWEETKINS, SWEETIKINS (or MISTER/MASTER/MISS/MS. SWEETKINS). In fairy tales, a child who has been switched in the cradle is neither a substituted heir nor a switcheroo (or switcheroonie), but the diminutive CHANGELING.

Contrasting connotations are another characteristic: an unenfranchised, powerless little child is also a LITTLE PRINCE or PRINCESS, a YOUNG LORD or LADY, and HIS or HER ROYAL HIGHNESS OF THE HIGH CHAIR. SIR or LADY plus a name or nickname causes endless delight: I have in my time known, and delighted in, several SIR HOTSHOTS and LADY LOVELIES.

One of the most amazing things about baby talk is that statements that ought to scare kids out of their wits pass without notice: "You're so cute I'm going to eat these toes, one at a time! Yum, yum, yum!" "I love you to pieces!" It is a credit to them that they are able to sort this out and reward such numbing idiocies with tolerant giggles.

Question: In the following essential list of high-chair endearments, how many terms do you suppose have made the great leap forward to adult love talk?

ANGEL, ANGEL BABY, ANGEL FACE, ANGEL PIE, BABY, BABYKINS, BIG EYES, BUNNYKINS, BUNNY NOSE, COOKIE, COOKIE FACE, DARLING, DEAR, DEARIE, DEAR HEART, DOLL,

FUNNY BUNNY, HONEY BUNCH, HONEY BUNNY, HONEY
PIE, LOVE, LOVELY LASSIE, SILLY BILLY, SNOOKUMS, SWEET-
HEART (or SWEET FACE), SWEETIE PIE.

Answer: All of them.

In English, babies do not have stomachs but TUM TUMS
or TUMMIES. An infant doesn't have buttocks either (thank
heavens! that word has always suggested, inexplicably, the
haunches of the bovine family to me); she or he has a BOT-
TOM, a BUM BUM, a HINY (diminutive for HIND END), a
TINY HINY, or—adapted into colloquial English from Yid-
dish—a TUSH or TUSHIE. Toes are LITTLE PIGGIES or TOOT-
SIES or TOOTSIE WOOTSIES. No child I know has a navel,
except at the doctor's office or when eating a certain kind of
orange. What they all have, however, are BELLY BUTTONS
(INNIES or OUTIES).

In a child's vocabulary, cats are KITTIES, dogs are DOG-
GIES, fish are FISHIES, worms can be WORMIES, birds are
BIRDIES, and even inanimate objects are their own kind of
cute: socks, for example, may become SOCKIES. (Among
adults, this neologism is known only among newlyweds.)
Naturally, if any of these things are small, they are ITSY
BITSY and TEENY WEENY. In generations past, little things
might be called WEE; today that word has lost its usefulness
as an adjective but, doubled up as WEE WEE, remains cur-
rent as a verb.

Farb says that the most common sounds in baby talk are
the consonants B, P, and M, followed by T, D, and N. BABA,

for example, can be a baby's word for himself (BABY) or for a pacifier or a milk bottle. The B sound also attaches by rhyme to almost anyone's name—MATTIE BATTIE, MIMI BIMI, MOMMY BOMMY and DADDY BADDY. A BOO is a dear or a darling, by itself or used as a suffix; the word may be a shortened form of BOOBY, a FOOL, in English since 1599 and derived from the Latin *balbus,* for "stammering." A modern reworking is BABBOO (feminine form: BAB-BOOETTE), from the "Peanuts" comic strip. Similar endearments fill the funny pages: Bill Watterson's BITSY POOKUM and POOGIE PIE in "Calvin and Hobbes," and Berkeley Breathed's PUDDIN' BUNS in "Outland."

A DOLL is a plaything, and a lover is not—but we like the word when we cuddle anyway. Usually we mean the perfectly made small replica of a baby, but those who read E. B. White's *Charlotte's Web* for their annual cleansing of pretension and sloppy phrasing know that a *doll* is also the smallest or pet pig of a litter, and it, too, can be an endearment. In 1560 *doll* referred to a low or common woman; one of Shakespeare's most robust (and bustiest, I suspect) characters is Doll Tearsheet, the innkeeper, whose last name hints of her special talents. In the American gangster patois concocted by Damon Runyon, the word refers to any desirable woman, but it's unisex today: one of my friends calls her husband, who towers over six feet tall, "DOLL."

Spinoffs include DOLL FACE ("Stick with me, DOLL FACE, and I'll make you a star"), DOLLY (also short for Dorothy), and BABY DOLL—an endearment, a style of shortie night-gown popularized in the 1950s, and a tad tainted by Holly-wood sex-kitten associations in the movie *Baby Doll*. The old-fashioned POPPET can be a puppet doll, a small dainty person, a darling or a pet—all of them suitable for lovespeak.

Entirely too adorable consonant substitutions occur when a letter like R is tough to pronounce; regrettably, classic baby talk includes WABBIT for RABBIT. Truth will out: parents (and lovers) have been known to add the UM sound with flagrant disregard to the sensibilities of passersby, producing such painful phrases as: WOULDUMS BABYWOVUMS WANT MORE MILKUMS? In a word: *ughums.*

Enough already!

Not everybody dotes on this stuff. Both babe-based dialects are an acquired taste, illogical babble, the opposite of thoughtful, measured communication. Baby talk is all feeling, all how said, not what said; a little can go too far very fast. In *Anecdotes,* Clifton Fadiman tells the story of Dr. Samuel Johnson, the legendary eighteenth-century dictionary maker and gloriously unapologetic grouch, who once offered a woman and her infant a lift in his coach on condition that she not use baby talk when addressing her child.

It was raining, and the woman gratefully accepted the ride and the rules. For a time a seemly, neoclassic harmony prevailed (just what the doctor ordered). But then the baby stirred, as babies do.

"The little dearie, is he going to open his eyesy-pysies then?" the mother murmured solicitously.

"Stop the coach!" Johnson bellowed. Within moments mother and child found themselves, once again, in the rain.

For adults pitching woo, the best advice on the subject of baby love talk is: go easy. Men and women who utter unctuous babyisms in front of anyone who does not adore them run the risk of ruin; if baby talk is a kind of test, those addressing the unbesotted will fail. In a Marx Brothers movie, Groucho takes a young woman for a boat ride on a lake. It's a pretty scene: ducks on the water, women in large hats, the rhythmic flash and dip of the oars. But she talks in a babyish, affected manner, and he—looking everywhere but at her, his eyebrows soaring, his cigar circling—asks after one of her lispy comments, "Was that you or the duck?"

Is something missing in this chapter? Yes. For all the FUNNY BUNNIES and DOLL FACES, there is another category of endearments that works equally well for the pram set and for paramours: the one connected to that other great primal drive, hunger. (As I know only too well: my son's first word was not "mama" or "dada," but "yotut," which meant yogurt, his favorite food.) It's another case of one vocabulary serving two passions: we speak what we love, we love what we need. Or, as Larry Parks and Jay Turnbow wrote in "Bread and Butter," a song made popular in 1964 by The Newbeats: "That's what my baby feeds me / I'm her lovin' man."

Yum! For more on the insatiable connection between food and loved ones of all ages, read on.

SEVEN FAMOUS LOVE PAIRS (IN ADDITION TO ROMEO AND JULIET) WHO DIED FOR LOVE

Hero and Leander
Pyramus and Thisbe
Antony and Cleopatra
Deirdre and Noise
Cathy and Heathcliff
Quasimodo and Esmeralda
Paolo and Francesca

POP QUIZ: Name two pairs who existed in real life.

(ANSWER: Antony and Cleopatra and Paolo and Francesca)

CHAPTER 5

LOVE BITES

OUCH? OR OOOOOHHH?

As every American teenager knows, a LOVE BITE, also known as a HICKEY or a MONKEY BITE, is one of those smudgy, soft bruises on the neck or shoulder that remains for all to see when a lover actually bites, or sucks, or presses really hard while kissing the aforementioned neck or shoulder. The presence of this kind of mark on another's neck sanctions giggles, leers, knowing stares, snorts, hoots, and any manner of rude remarks younger siblings, classmates, and coworkers can devise in their tiny little brains. Wedded bliss is no protection: married people are known to produce these marks on their partners just before the kissed spouse is scheduled to make a major presentation or lecture a class of adolescents on a serious subject.

Why do we bite one another? Why do we laugh about it? What do biting and eating have to do with love?

In nouns, adjectives, adverbs, and attitudes, food has everything to do with love and always has, as proverbs prove: "The way to a man's heart is through his stomach."

"There is no sincerer love than the love of food." "Cooking, like love, should be entered into with abandon or not at all." Would Adam have given up Eden if Eve had proffered not an apple but a lottery ticket? Or universal health care? Or a great novel?

Food and love are as irrevocably mixed as sensuality and love, probably because a baby's first love contacts and sensual pleasures arrive at the same moment, from the mother at feeding time. Like lovemaking, eating satisfies a natural, necessary urge. It's no surprise that we take the yen and yearning for foodstuff, along with the vocabulary, right into the yin and yanging of adult pleasures. In the kitchen and in the bedroom, it's not what we say—exactly—but what we mean. And what we remember.

A toddler in her mother's arms is A REAL DUMPLING of a girl; so too is a curvaceous twenty-two-year-old SEXPOT, which is no doubt the best pot for simmering desire. Love objects may look YUMMY and have a SAUCY glance. We HUNGER for love itself, for a lover's proximity, for a smile, a kiss, a look, a gesture. We SMACK our lips in anticipation of good food or good kissing. We TASTE or NIBBLE or SUCK or LICK a sweetheart's ears, fingertips, or—as in the case of a certain British duchess in the summer of 1991—toes. We can be STARVED FOR LOVE unless we get our FILL OF LOVE.

Here is a bill of fare of delicious love words:

APPLE

This round and firm fruit suggests a young woman's breasts; one bit of sensuous (and symbolic) gormandizing suggests that, halved, it neatly depicts the female genitalia. Whole, its circular shape also symbolizes the completeness and totality of love. Like passion, the apple is too often a "forbidden" or troublesome commodity: not only did it trigger the first couple's expulsion from Paradise, but a golden apple lies at the heart of what caused the Trojan War.

It happened at *the* social event of the eon, a wedding, when the powers that were chose the noble Trojan Paris to award a golden apple to the "most beautiful" goddess present. He gave it to Aphrodite, because she offered what seemed to him the best bribe: the love of Helen, the most beautiful woman on earth. The other goddesses present, Athena and Hera, were not pleased. (It wasn't the bribery that bothered them—they had offered him skill as a warrior and greatness, respectively.) So they took sides as only mythological deities can when Menelaus, Helen's husband, objected to her kidnapping. One thing led to another, war ensued, and the rest is the *Iliad.*

The APPLE OF MY EYE is a nonsexual endearment: the pupil of the eye was compared to an apple in the Bible because of its shape, and the apple of one's eye is as precious as eyesight. An APPLE DUMPLING is an edible darling, and

APPLE PIE is a symbol of mother love as well as all things American.

BISCUIT

This old endearment, a noun once used in the sense of DELICIOUS LITTLE MORSEL, has been reborn as an adjective on college campuses in the 1990s, as in "He looks really BISCUIT in a suit."

COOKIE, COOKIE FACE

A less sexual term of affection than YOU'RE THE CREAM IN MY COFFEE, CREAM PUFF, CRUMPET, A NICE TIDY MORSEL, A TASTY BIT, A REAL CUPCAKE (perhaps because women's brassieres have "cups"), this endearment fairly reeks of domestic harmony.

HONEY

A love name since medieval times, its sweet alternatives include HON, HONEY FACE, HONEY PIE. A HONEY MAN is a male lover. Honey comes from bees, those insects we discuss with children, along with the birds, when we want to explain sex to them without mentioning it. Bees do have something to do with propagation: you might call them the engines of love when it comes to transporting flower pollen.

A HONEYMOON, according to Dr. Samuel Johnson, who harrumphed and sneered his wordy, wise way through the eighteenth century, is the first month after marriage, a honeyed period of wedded bliss. After that, just as the moon wanes to a mere sliver of reflected light, it is the nature of marriage to diminish in sweetness. Too much sweetness palls: Lord Byron characterized his miserable first weeks with Anne Isabella Milbanke, whom he married and abandoned in 1815, as TREACLEMOON.

For those who intend to be married longer than twenty-eight days, the moon will wax full again, just as love well observed renews itself. The contemporary honeymoon is the vacation time (a week, ten days, a weekend) taken by newlyweds after marriage. (Inexplicably, many home-town newspapers in America report honeymoon news in the passive voice: "A wedding trip was taken by the couple to Club Riot, where the nude beach was visited daily.")

L. M. Boyd, a columnist for *The San Francisco Chronicle,* says that HONEYMOON comes from a candle-making process used by medieval clergymen, who "harvested" wax from beehives. At first, he claims, the honey was *only a by-product;* the religious, ever resourceful and wishing of course neither to waste nor to want, used it to make an intoxicating drink called mead. They served it at weddings and it was, in a word, a smash. As a result, the "post-ceremony time became known as the Month of Honey."

PEACH

A very attractive woman is a PEACH, perhaps because she has a peaches-and-cream complexion, and a peach is a good, rare discovery in any walk of life: "He was a peach of a boss." "She was a peach of a mother-in-law." *Peachy keen.*

PIE

As a suffix, this substantive noun indicates a critical mass of the yummy item specified: HONEY PIE, SWEETIE PIE, LOVEY PIE, CUTIE PIE, ANGEL PIE.

PUMPKIN

Sometimes shortened to PUNKIN or fancied up as PUMPKIN FACE, this loving term bangs the gong of lovers' idiocy once again: why a fat, rough-skinned orange vegetable is appealing beats me, but it is.

SUGAR

Either as a noun in direct address, or as an adjective after a lover's first name, or as a redoubled endearment (SUGAR, MICHAEL SUGAR, SUGAR PIE), this term of love gets sprinkled all over the place.

TOMATO

In slang, a juicy, ripe woman, as described by an admiring man. She might also be a DISH, and either a male or a female can be DISHY (not to be confused with *dis,* noun or verb, which is current teen talk for "disrespect," "criticism," or "criticize").

Food is fun, but in love language excess does not always equal success. In *The Last Lion,* his biography of Winston Churchill, William Manchester quotes a love letter written by a rival British statesman and ladies' man. On this occasion, circa 1918, the man's mistress had mentioned that she was hungry. His reply:

> *When I woke up at 6 my first thought was of the loving little face engraved on my heart & I had a fierce thought to go there & then cover it with kisses. But darling I am jealous once more. I know your thoughts are on roast mutton & partridge & chicken & potatoes & that you are longing to pass them through the lips which are mine & to bite them with the luscious joy with the dazzling white teeth that I love to press. I know that today I am a little out of it & that your heart is throbbing of other thrills. . . .*
>
> *Your very jealous old Lover*

The lessons this letter teaches are: (a) it is possible to overdo food metaphors when searching for endearments; (b) the menu is all wrong: it should have been champagne mousse instead of mutton, parfaits instead of potatoes; (c) gluttony is not attractive, and food is not—no matter what gourmands say—exactly the same as sex; (d) love letters should be taken with a grain of salt.

APHRODISIACS are those seductive love potions, elixirs, and yummy sweetmeats named for the Greek goddess of love, Aphrodite. They give edible credibility to love, or at least suggest its great and good friend, lust. The mere mention of aphrodisiacs raises eyebrows. It also raises the hopes of many older women, and the spirits if not the physiological *ne plus ultra* (that's *penis* to you unromantic moderns) of many older men.

In plain English, aphrodisiacs are foodstuffs, sometimes rather doubtful foodstuffs, that people believe will compel, cause, induce, or otherwise enhance physical passion. There are aphrodisiacs for both sexes, but most seem geared for female preparation and male consumption. For sexually adventurous women yoked by marriage or habit to one of the many men struck down, down, down at age seventy by an alarming epidemic of what they all say is back trouble, they are—well, they are welcome. If we are to believe the Cavalier poet Robert Herrick's lyric "To His Mistresses," written in the seventeenth century, men themselves may be most grateful:

> *Help me! help me! now I call*
> *To my pretty witchcrafts all;*
> *Old I am, and cannot do*
> *That I was accustomed to.*
> *Bring your magics, spells, and charms,*
> *To enflesh my thighs and arms;*
> *Is there no way to beget*
> *In my limbs their former heat?*
> *Aeson had, as poets feign,*
> *Baths that made him young again:*
> *Find that medicine, if you can,*
> *For your dry, decrepit man*
> *Who would fain his strength renew,*
> *Were it but to pleasure you.*

Culinary clues to coitus fill scores of books. Most simply, an aphrodisiac—(the word remains alluring as long as we forget that *aphro* refers to the foam that roiled up around the severed genitals of the ancient god Uranus when Aphrodite was born from the sea)—is anything at all that a person associates with love or sensual pleasure.

It might be a magnum of champagne. It could be, as Cleopatra demonstrated to the astonished Antony, a pearl dissolved in wine. According to one report, a famous Chinese general believed that a meal of black chow dog was perfect for precoital consumption. In *A Midsummer Night's Dream,* it is the juice of a certain plant known to Oberon:

> *Yet mark'd I where the bolt of Cupid fell.*
> *It fell upon a little Western flower,*
> *Before milk-white, now purple with love's wound,*
> *And maidens call it love-in-idleness.*
>
> —*II, i, 165 ff.*

Do people love chocolate? It is a favorite gift on St. Valentine's Day, and serious lovers (of chocolate and each other) insist that it has in it phenylethylalamine ait, a chemical researchers say also exists in the brains of people in love. (I'm sure there's a good scientific answer to this, yet one can't help but wonder: How do they know it's in the brain? How did they extract this substance? Were the lovers still alive? If not, is this proof that love survives death? Did the scientists know *for sure* that the subjects were truly in love, or were they just on the make? If alive, were the lovers feeling mostly love, lust, or terror when the chemical was removed?)

For hundreds of years, people believed or suspected that the shape of a food indicated in some way its power or force. Not to be confused with other symbolic shapes of love, like a Valentine heart or Cupid's bow and arrow, the shapes associated with aphrodisiacs were strictly genital: round shapes like a breast or buttock, and long, firm shapes like a penis rampant.

Besides the apples and cleft peaches, there was the man-drake, or Mandragora officinarum: a member of the night-shade family (which includes tomatoes and eggplant). Its roots are long and—according to legend—resemble the lower limbs of a human. The old wives' tale that follows it through countless footnotes is that the mandrake "shrieked" when it was dug up. The most famous lines in English about this oddly compelling plant are in John Donne's "Song":

> *Go, and catch a falling star,*
> *Get with child a mandrake root.*

The juicier the aphrodisiac, the better. Melons are sexy, and can refer to women's breasts—as do plump tomatoes, succulent pears, and sun-warmed nectarines. In fact, the garden is, to the discerning eye, just bursting with eroticism: there's phallic asparagus, tumescent zucchini, and oodles of small, round or saclike fruits—figs, anyone?—that are potentially powerful because they grow best in torrid climes, and their shape suggests male genitalia. Europeans were excited, or wanted to be, when the potato was discovered in the New World because they thought the rock-shaped vegetable would increase sexual potency. (Actually, only some of them thought that. French peasants thought potatoes might cause leprosy.)

Other sexy edibles over the years have been oysters, clams, caviar, eggs, and the ground-up horns and tusks of fierce animals like the rhinoceros. Just about any penile-shaped root, which is to say just about any root, was supposed to be good for potency. According to a seventeenth-century health guide, *The Complete Herbal,* orchid roots were supposed to strengthen "the genital parts."

Today's lovers are no less susceptible to the promise of prowess; when nutrition began to make headlines during the 1970s, vitamin E got a reputation (the way a high school girl can get a reputation) as a cure for male impo-

SIX WELL-ROOTED SYMBOLS OF LOVE

All manner of roses
(except the yellow rose, which signals infidelity)
Tulips
Honeysuckle
Mistletoe
Orange blossoms
Myrtle

tence. In 1990, *East/West* magazine ran a special section on aphrodisiacs, mostly of Chinese and Asian invention. Some of the items recommended for the sex menu: ginseng root, deer-horn shavings, wild carrot (Queen Anne's lace), and seahorses. (You read it right the first time.)

What most concoctors of chewable desire may overlook is that language—which gives a name for all the foods we know—is the greatest aphrodisiac. Love, like laughter, can be triggered by the imagination in action—just the sort of thing language strives to achieve all the time. Consider the menu of images and associations brought to mind in these lines from Andrew Marvell's poem "The Garden" and to what purpose they might be put:

> *What wondrous life is this I lead!*
> *Ripe apples drop about my head;*
> *The luscious clusters of the vine*
> *Upon my mouth do crush their wine;*
> *The nectarine and curious peach*
> *Into my hands themselves do reach;*
> *Stumbling on melons as I pass,*
> *Ensnared with flowers, I fall on grass.*

Who wouldn't?

Suppose, in the best tradition of imaginary, daydream seductions, you plan a perfect picnic lunch for lovers. Will it include: Hearty meat-loaf sandwiches on whole-wheat toast with mayonnaise and ketchup? Or daintily sliced, pinkly rare roast beef on sweetly fragrant rye bread with French mustard? Cottage cheese or caviar? Raisin-oatmeal cookies or chocolate mousse? Soda pop or champagne?

Some meals have romance and some don't. Just the mention of certain foods—the word CHOCOLATE, for example—can cause extraordinary reactions in otherwise staid human beings: rolled eyes; giggles; low, hummimg, slurpy sounds; protestations; capitulations; unabashed and voluble expressions of sensual expectation. As any cookbook collector knows, menus and preparation words are provocative. Cooks BLEND, BOIL, CODDLE, COMBINE, CREAM, DRIZZLE, FOLD (and FOLD GENTLY), HEAT, MIX, SAUTÉ, SIMMER, SPICE, STEAM, STIR, STREW, and TASTE.

Sexy food—the real stuff, available at the market, not the nonexistent nostrums of myth or the exotica that might involve stripping a tree of its bark—embodies a world in which fantasy merges with gustatory reality. There are no rules here, but three certain recommendations.

One: Romantic, pleasing platefuls are (or should seem to be) a little strange or unusual (but never repulsive), a distinct and memorable sensual pleasure.

Two: In food-filled love language, foreign phrases or references work magic.

Three: In selecting "such stuff as dreams are made on,"

romantic foods (except chocolate) are either red or pink in color.

Here is a list of altogether available food and drink suitable for consumption in the altogether.

RED EDIBLES

Roast beef and roast lamb, both rare. Red snapper. Salmon. Shrimp.

Red-leafed artichoke. Red leaf lettuce. Certain herb teas. Radicchio. Radishes. Red bell pepper. Red onion. Tomatoes (plum, beefsteak).

Apples, raw and juicy, with cheese and wine, or baked with cinnamon and butter and eaten in front of an open fire, or sliced, sprinkled with lemon, and popped in a pie for the domestic touch. Cherries. Cranberries. Plums. Raspberries. Red grapes: biologically, seeds are sexy, but when practicing the consuming art, seedless red grapes are more seductive (and less likely to get caught between the teeth). Rhubarb (as in rhubarb pie). Ruby red grapefruit. Sicilian blood oranges. Strawberries.

And there is a class all its own of uninhibitors: Bloody Mary cocktails, Campari, grenadine, Framboise liqueur, pink Champagnes, red wines, and rosé wines.

Red foods that are *not* sexy include red beans, beets, red cabbage, and red potatoes—unless, of course, these happen to be the favorite foods of one's lover (*de gustibus non disputandum,* which can be roughly translated as *different strokes for different folks*).

A VALENTINE'S DAY DINNER FOR TWO

Ice Cold Champagne
(very dry, served with a sliced strawberry in
a gold-dipped flute)
Caviar
(with minced onion, hard-boiled egg
and lemon, on toast points)
Filet Mignon
Whole Steamed Artichokes, Hollandaise Sauce
Chocolate Soufflé
Coffee

If, on the off chance, it happens that you don't have time to prepare this meal, do the following:

Send children, if any, to the babysitter's house. Light candles. Take the phone off the hook (or set the answering machine to answer silently). Put the beepers in the closet under last year's mufflers. Order Chinese take-out. Read the above menu out loud.

Speak low.

Speak love.

INTERLUDE

ONE NIGHT, when Henry VIII of England was between courses at a banquet, those who fawned and feared in the royal presence invented a new entertainment: the Interlude, or what we moderns call a skit.

Some interludes were heavy stuff, written and performed in Latin, laden from here to Eternity with righteous reminders. Many, many more, performed in "vulgar" everyday English and song, were designed to provoke knowing laughter and elbows in the ribs (but not the King's ribs!)— in short, to guarantee the sort of evening that blurs detail but is remembered as a success. Interludes were the ancestors of vaudeville, "Your Show of Shows," and "Saturday Night Live."

A favorite theme was the long-fought, never-won battle of the sexes. Notes French scholar Francois Laroque in *The*

Age of Shakespeare (failing to shroud what was clearly uproarious, outrageous behavior in dusty, academic language): "Closely related to the morality plays were the interludes, short dramas that were performed between the courses of a banquet. They frequently took the form of long debates on the subject of marriage, punctuated by often obscene or scatological comic scenes acted by clowns known as 'vices.' "

Ah sweet mystery of vice, at last we find you—"closely related," as you must be, to moral matters. Interludes tootled along on ditties that plumbed the depths of ribaldry with suggestive lyrics, puns, and pratfalls. The philosophy was simplistic, the characters constant, the resolution fatalistic capitulation.

As these are intercoursal delights, we take as inspiration the first line of *Twelfth Night:* "If music be the food of love, play on." So I present here, in a brief interlude, a medley of song titles that tell a story—the usual story, but that's the point. Hint to textual deconstructionists: the punctuation is mine, as are the interpolated words, and it's not about *sex* but *love.*

INTERAMORE: AN INTERLUDE IN FOUR PARTS

SCENE: The back seat of a Chevy, whereon a tangle of lithe limbs grasp, clutch, push, and pull. Outside it is a night of starry sky and a full-blown moon that resembles an Oreo cookie when you take a chocolate side off to lick the white frosting. Music on the car radio fades to background noise as the arms and legs part to reveal the rumpled but still clothed forms of ADAM and EVELYN, he bulging below the waist, she above.

EVELYN: "Stop! in the name of love."

ADAM: "Why shouldn't I?" "There's yes, yes in your eyes."

EVELYN: "There is more to love."

ADAM: "What's love got to do with it?"

EVELYN: "I'd like you to love me." My friends, "they say it's wonderful."

ADAM: "Yatata, yatata, yatata"! "Say, say say"! What I say is, "you're the one that I want."

EVELYN: "When I discovered you," "my darling," "I got the feeling," "I remember it well": I sang "I feel love," "I feel free," "I feel pretty." But "when you're away," "I still remember you." "You've done something to my heart." "It amazes me" "everytime you touch me." "What more do you want?"

ADAM: "I want you," "I want to be bad." "Fun, fun, fun," "thighs and whispers."

EVELYN: "Don't."

ADAM: "Take it easy," "I can't help myself." "I want your sex."

EVELYN: "Take me home."

ADAM: "What'd I say?"

EVELYN: "What do you think I am?"

ADAM: "Kiss me honey, honey, kiss me."

EVELYN: "Don't kiss me again."

ADAM: "It's a perfect relationship." "Don't fight it."

EVELYN: "No love, no nothin'."

ADAM: "Come on." "Do, do, do."

EVELYN: "How come you do me like you do?" "Friends"—"they're all getting married but me." "I want what I want when I want it"—"love and marriage." "Make me the woman that you go home to."

ADAM: "Don't fence me in."

EVELYN: *(Takes the flower from her breast and throws it at him.)* "This orchid means good-bye," "because" "I've been loving you too long." "I just don't like this kind of living." "It's late." "I'm going home." *(She jumps out of the car and walks off stage, then returns, hands on hips.)* "I'll get over you." *(Exit.)*

Lights dim, then go out as ADAM remains in the car, looking flabbergasted. After a moment, a spot comes up on EVELYN, sitting on a bench, combing her hair or doing another intimate bit of stage business that indicates a *pensive mood.*

EVELYN: "Am I blue?" "Love on the rocks" makes me sad. "My defenses are down." "I just can't help believing" "love changes everything." "He's sure the boy I love." "I'm building up to an awful letdown." "If he really knew me," he'd be "head over heels in love," "be-cause" "I'm a lover not a fighter." "I believe" "love is the reason," "life's desire." "Love changes everything." "Love" means "to have and to hold." "That's all I need." Oh, Adam, "when will you say 'I love you'?"

Spot fades to black over EVELYN and rises on ADAM, whom we find pacing in front of the Chevy.

ADAM: "Oh woman, oh why?" "What'll I do?" "When I'm with you," Evie, "when you're in my arms," "it's magic." "I know that you know" "there's no time like the present." "I love you." "Friends"? "They all say I'm the biggest fool." They say, "once bitten, twice shy." "I remember" "Nadine." And "Jolene." Not to mention "come on Eileen." "Still," "maybe this time . . ." "I guess I'll have to change my plan." "I can't explain," but "I love her."

Lights fade to black, go up on EVELYN. ADAM approaches, flowers in hand.

ADAM: "Hello, baby." *(Evelyn says nothing, and he shifts awkwardly from one foot to another.)* "Where do I begin?"
EVELYN: "Don't."
ADAM: "Hey, good lookin'," "it's no secret I love you."
EVELYN: "It's too late." "I don't want to talk about it."
ADAM: "We mustn't say good-bye."

EVELYN: "That's what you think." "I get along without you very well."

ADAM: "Listen to me."

EVELYN: *(Turns to look at him for the first time.)* "It better be good."

ADAM: "Life is peculiar." "Little by little" "I saw the light." "I'll never find another you." "I nearly let love go slipping through my fingers," but "I could be happy with you."

EVELYN: "That's all?" "There's gotta be something better than this."

ADAM: "I'm shy," but "the words are in my heart." "I mean to say," "I'd like you to love me." "I can't tell why I love you but I do." "Yeh, yeh," "I'm no angel," "I'm only human after all." "Still," "you are my destiny." "We're gonna work it out."

EVELYN: *(To herself, musing.)* "I may be crazy but I love you." *(Squares her shoulders, faces him.)* "I never heard you say" "if it's love.". . .

ADAM: "If I could . . ."

EVELYN: "Say the word."

ADAM: "I surrender, dear." "I love you 1000 times."

EVELYN: "You wouldn't fool me, would you?"

ADAM: "Baby, baby," "I want a girl like you." "You are my heart's delight."

EVELYN: "I can't say no."

ADAM: "You can depend on me." *(Adam kisses Evelyn with prolonged gusto.)* "Let's get it on." "Say you will."

EVELYN: *(Sighs happily.)* "I'll never have to dream again."

ADAM: "My love," "my life." "Maybe I'm amazed"— "I'm in love," "I'm on fire." "It's ecstasy when you lay down next to me." "What more do you want?"

EVELYN: *(Embracing him passionately.)* "I wanna get married."

ADAM: "All right": "Will you marry me?"

EVELYN: "Yes, indeed." "I'll be your everything." "I'll never let you go."

ADAM: "You've got that look."

EVELYN: "You've got that thing."

ADAM: "What a perfect combination"!

EVELYN: "Wow!"

(They collapse into another tangle of lithe, long limbs as the lights dim, then go black.)

FINIS

ANIMAL URGES

Birds do it. Bees do it.
Even educated fleas do it.
—COLE PORTER, "LET'S DO IT," 1928

NIMAL IMAGES suit feelings of love just fine—they admit primitive, basic, simply sensational lust but tame it, too, with affection and absurdity. Sex fascinates. It feels good.

It's also scary. It has nothing to do with thinking, the talent that we claim, we *insist,* sets us "above" the animals—and not incidentally protects us from the vicissitudes of nature and other unruly forces. We live by rules (even if we make them up as we go along); animals, including the animal within, don't. How exciting! How unpredictable! How dangerous! How thrilling! How to manage?

So love finds a CAGE, a LAIR, a NEST, a SWINGING VINE, an airy AERIE or TREETOP HIDEAWAY to call its own in this natural wilderness of dangerous animal urges. We often let animal images do the talking, for in the peculiar, slurpy mix of sex, sweetness, sensation, seduction, and sensitivity, they bridge the potentially abysmal gap between the vaulting, vaunted intellect and the earthy instincts.

Essential sexual animalia is most audible in popular music. There's Paul Anka's "Puppy Love" (1960), the "Elusive Butterfly" of Bob Lind (1966), and the appalling "Muskrat Love" sung by Captain and Tennille in 1976. Natural warblers do the most tuneful lovemaking: in the top hundred popular songs about animals compiled by Fred Brower, twenty-four are about birds, including three robins and three doves. The allure of the wild also found memorable expression among the Troggs and their defining moment on the pop charts in 1966: "Wild thing, I think I love you,/But I want to knoooooow for sure." I'm sure the wild thing's mother was pleased as could be.

In everyday love parlance, there are TIGERS, and fuzzy-wuzzy PUSSYCATS and KITTENS. There are still sweethearts like the one described in *Wily Beguiled,* a play of 1606: "Sweet Peg . . . My honey, my bunny, my duck, my dear." A GRRRRRR in the morning is not always a growl. Ann Landers once ran a letter from a man who boasted that he called his wife "Kri Kri," the name Dwight D. Eisenhower gave to his pet goat. It's all to be expected when beast meets beauty in coital bliss; if we need euphemisms and indirection almost as much as we need sex, this particular set of images fits so naturally that it follows like morning after the night before.

The Roman orator Cicero said, "Simia quam similis,

turpissima bestia, nobis!"—how like the APE, vilest of beasts, we are! Alas, it's only too true. At least one ape specializes in rape; among the orangutans, animals blessed with four hands instead of two hands and two feet, males use the extra two opposable thumbs and their superior weight to force sexual relations with females. More often apes are just primitive: we say a person GOES APE over another when we mean he is uncontrollably attracted to someone else.

A brawny BEAR can be tamed by love into a huggable armful. Two influential love bears are largely responsible for this belief—stuffed TEDDY BEARS (named after Theodore Roosevelt), and WINNIE-THE-POOH or POOH BEAR (the creation in poetry and prose of A. A. Milne), who loves honey, a staple of endearments. Ursine appeal shows no sign of letting up. Bearish endearments include (NAME OF YOUR LOVED ONE) BEAR, HONEY BEAR, DADDY BEAR, FUZZY BEAR, ANGEL BEAR, with the clear implication that those so dubbed are also powerful and warm, especially when hibernating.

Sound a meow, now, for the formidable felines, maligned and mysterious, always misunderstood (but then, do they care?). By itself, CAT is a negative term for a woman given to making unkind remarks, usually about other women. She is also capable of playing with a lover as if he were a toy (or, to stick to the theme, a small, furry rodent). The LION is a predator and hunter with formidable sexual capacities. Lovers who are LEOPARDS or PANTHERS, however, are even more dangerous—strong, silent, slim types, deliciously ruthless. Best of all is the TIGER, who is deadly but dear, too, and able to "soothe a savage breast" in himself and his mate. A woman of frank sexuality may be a TIGRESS, especially if she purrs when pleased, sports long fingernails (preferably blood red), and is known to growl encouragements like "C'mere tiger," or "Let's go, tiger."

KITTENS and KITTIES can scratch but they really aren't scary: this is primitive desire in a manageable size, equipped to snarl and slash but domesticated to the twitch of their tails. To be KITTENISH is to be adorable: "She was all girlishness and wildness, playfulness and kittenish" (Dickens, *Martin Chuzzlewit,* 1844). *Pussy,* short for *pussycat,* has been around since 1583 and—rather oddly—the shortened *puss* is slang for face.

Language books are made for moments like this: even when not thinking the impolite, there is genuine confusion about *pussy,* mostly a mix—I'm not making this up—of cats and carrying cases. To wit, we know that the first kind of *pussy* is *puss* plus a diminutive ending, an endearment for real animals, either four- or two-footed; *puss* appears in several Teutonic languages as well as Gaelic, and it may have evolved from a common call to cats, a *"puss, puss, puss"* equivalent to *"Here, kitty, kitty, kitty."* The other *pussy* is perhaps, as the dictionary suggests delicately, of Low German or Scandinavian origin, akin to *puss,* meaning *pocket* in Old Norse, and *puse* (or *vulva*) in Low German. It got Englished as *pusa,* or *bag,* in Old English. This can be love language (see chapter 3), but take care.

Ah, sweet birds of youth! BIRDS are sexy, and always have been, probably because flying is a natural metaphor for sexual RAPTURE (a word that shares the same Latin root as *rape.*) In medieval times, even the mild-mannered sparrow was a symbol of lechery. True lovebirds are DOVES; turtledoves symbolize peace and are known for COOING. The phrase BILLING AND COOING, hundreds of years old in English, likens fowl lovemaking to the whispered sighs and light kisses of people pleasing people. Larks are sexy because they sing in the morning. Nightingales are sexy because they sing at night.

(However, those who limit their romantic nightingale reading to Keats's *Ode* get only half the story, and the more modern, romantic half at that, for in the darkness favored by the nightingale—in an ancient tale that puts the violent saga of John and Lorena Bobbitt in classic perspective—the dangers of wild lechery run rampant. In Greek myth, Tereus, son of the war god Ares and ruler of Thrace, helped the King of Attica put down some civil unrest; in return he was given the hand of the king's daughter, Procne, who bore him a son, Itys. The details are a little murky: Tereus either stashed his wife in the country and told everyone she was dead and then married her sister, Philomela, or merely allowed Procne to have Philomela come to visit. Either way, he "dishonored" Philomela, ripped out her tongue so she couldn't tell, and deserted her; returning home, he told Procne she was dead.

But Philomela was clever and determined; she wove the truth into cloth, made a robe of it, and sent it to Procne. Finding herself beyond simple rage, the wronged wife killed Itys, cooked him, and served him to her unfaithful husband that night for dinner. Tereus identified the entrée only *after* he had consumed it; brutal to the last, he snatched up an axe and pursued his wife, who had fled to her sister. Finally, answering the women's prayers, the gods ended this nasty domestic dispute by turning them all into birds: Tereus became a hoopoe (or, in some versions, a hawk), Procne a swallow, and Philomela a nightingale, which means "lover of song." Some song, some robe, some love symbol.

Barnyard COCKS stand for insolence in medieval literature, but that's not all: the term has been common slang for penis since 1618, and (like some men) cocks are known to crow of their accomplishments—which, for roosters at least, amount to little more than getting up early in the morning (though for some cocks past their prime the accomplishment might deserve celebration). As Marian Evans Cross, also known as George Eliot, wrote in *Adam Bede* in 1859, "He was like a cock who thought the sun had risen to hear him crow." The romantic ribaldry of the word goes back further: in the anonymous poem "I Have a Gentle Cock" from the fifteenth century, the cock is a much adored pet:

His eyen are of crystal
Locken all in amber;
And every night he percheth him
In my lady's chamber.

These days, the word BIRDS is on the endangered species list of love words, as young women who arrived in America with British rockers in the 1960s flourished, then faded as the label turned dismissive, even contemptuous. The term, though rare nowadays, still means an available young woman, roughly equivalent to CHICK and sometimes confused with GROUPIE. BIRD is also slang for penis, but to FLIP THE BIRD is not a complimentary gesture. As feathered creatures go, CHICK sounds so cool, so hip, so modern. So surprise! It's been an endearment for a young girl since 1610. These days it means a sexy young female, and is frequently modified by HOT, COOL, or SWINGIN'. It is probably a short form of CHICKEN, an old endearment; in *Macbeth*, Macduff calls his children "all my pretty chickens."

CHICKADEE, an American word for the crestless titmouse since 1838, is a less sexual term of endearment for either sex.

Fowl of a different sort—DUCK, DUCKS, or DUCKIES—predate CHICKS as endearments, first appearing in print in 1590. A DUCK is a darling or a dear; Partridge and Beale cite this explanation from Richard Steele's *The Tender Husband* in 1705:

Niece: So, my savage—
Aunt: O fie, no more of that to your husband, Biddy.
Hump: No matter, I like it as well as duck or love—

The endearment can be used for men or women today, even though technically male ducks are drakes. These wild high fliers frequently come with an adjective: *dear, darling, sweet,* and—in former times—*dainty* (or *daynte*). In the nineteenth century, a superlative form was DUCK OF DIAMONDS, used by Dickens in *The Old Curiosity Shop.* As for GEESE, those beautiful babblers are notoriously stupid, at least in folk-

FIVE FEMALE CHARACTERS
WHO LOVED AND LOST

Medea
The Duchess of Malfi
Anna Karenina
Oenone, wife of Paris
The first Mrs. Rochester

lore, so a lover can tease by calling his (or her) object of affection a *silly goose* (though the limited appeal of this loving derogation disappears entirely for those who have had occasion to follow in the muck-littered path of these creatures). *To goose* a loved one (that is, poke her fanny) is impolite and might result in a call to the police. In *Henry IV, Part I,* Lady Percy calls the heroic Hotspur, her husband, a GIDDY GOOSE when he becomes amorous. (Well, they do have long necks.)

The barnyard abounds in love creatures. The word BUN-NIES has been with us since 1690—according to Eugene T. Maleska in *The Pleasure of Words,* it's a "lengthening" of the word BUN, Scottish dialect for rabbit's tail. In American slang, we know that BUNS is a euphemism for buttocks, usually male, but BUNNIES are cuddly—be they little animals or big girls. Sex may be scary, but not with a BEACH BUNNY (young female Homo sapiens in bikini) or a SNOW BUNNY (novice skier, often nubile). HONEY BUNNY comes from the nursery; it works at precious (in all senses of the word) moments. The BUNNY HUG, less overwhelming than a BEAR HUG, is a popular dance performed as couples embrace, a clinch in motion.

We all know LAMB, LAMBY-PIE, LAMBY-POO, and LAMB-KINS—soft, warm, saccharine creatures, also said to be gentle and faithful and, in human form, extremely trying to the mature lover. Likewise, mice may make women scream, but Hamlet rebukes his mother for letting her new husband make love to her and "call you his MOUSE." Another, more typically favorable example cited in *Brewer's Dictionary of Phrase and Fable:*

> *"God bless you, mouse," the bridegroom said,*
> *And smakt her on the lips.*

—*WARNER*, ALBION'S ENGLAND, *II, X, 1592*

Are PIGS cute? Maybe. In E. B. White's *Charlotte's Web* they even attain simple nobility. But are pigs sexy? PIGSNEY, literally a "pig's eye," was a love term first used by Chaucer; it means darling, a pet—usually female. A PINKENY, which sounds to twentieth-century ears like an eye inflammation, meant a small, pig-sized eye six hundred years ago and was also, incredibly, an endearment then. POOCH or POOCHIE, American slang for *puppy,* is much more popular as an endearment, but a DOG is a loser.

Among unreconstructed male chauvinists, an attractive and lively young woman is a FILLY. The usual adjectives: *flighty, frisky,* the ever useful *dainty,* and *skittish.* That the purpose of a healthy young filly was to bear riders and, later, bear foals is the point of this term. Today the word, used in the first sense, still occurs in porn film titles. The male equivalent is STALLION, implying virility and strength, occasionally (deplorably) modified by the word ITALIAN by desperate sports commentators.

A FOX, on the other hand, enters the barnyard for a purpose, and a two-legged one is an attractive, sexually interesting woman. FOXY means sexy or attractive femininity, used of a woman who is aware of her allure and probably experienced.

There are animals we should avoid, in language and in love. Literally, a BITCH is a female dog. Colloquially she is a loud, obnoxious, disagreeable, ill-mannered woman; this is never a loving term. A man who is as ruthless, smart, and indefatigable in his hunt for female sexual conquests is a WOLF. A WOLF WHISTLE is the three-note whistled appreciation of female good looks, usually emitted on the street to signal that there's a sexy woman on the horizon and the whistler's hormones are functioning, just in case hers are too. A bit of the BEAST can excite, but one of the crudest phrases of Shakespeare is Iago's report to Brabantio in *Othello* that "your daughter and the Moor are now making the beast with two backs" (I, i, 116–118). Courtship, even when strained through scintillating intellect, is often animalistic: in *Much Ado About Nothing,* Shakespeare's lovers Beatrice and Benedick fly at each other incessantly, waging verbal war. Of course they are in love; the hostility provides an outlet for the nervous alarm they feel as passion engulfs logic.

Darwinians explain this behavior as a kind of testing: each creature is just making sure the other is of fine enough mettle to bear the genetic standard. But then Darwinians can explain love, too: it takes newborn humans so long, fifteen years at least, to get big enough to fend for themselves and, in their turn, to procreate that—for the surest success in evolution—human parents have to stay together a long time (about two *years* for every minute they spend actually getting the sperm to the egg—not counting foreplay, of course).

The blend of romance and rut is a touchy, uneasy one, perhaps best explained in the deliberately cool, abstract language of the psychologist. Carl Jung wrote in *The Psychology of the Unconscious* in 1943:

> *The erotic instinct is something questionable, and will always be so whatever a future set of laws may have to say on the matter. It belongs, on the one hand, to the original animal nature of man, which will exist as long as man has an animal body. On the other hand it is connected with the highest forms of the spirit. But it blooms only when spirit and instinct are in true harmony.*

Our animal-inspired love words—all the HONEY BEARS and KITTENS and TIGERS and even some BIG APES—may wrap an indulgent, unrealistic glow around the facts of life, but they suggest, also, that we are on our way in these present times to a benign and tolerant acceptance of our animal natures. The trick—and it is always a bit like magic—is to keep the physical and the intellectual halves of our being in balance. As the novelist Julian Barnes once said, "Love is just a system for getting someone to call you darling after sex."

Good system.

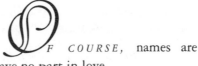

WHAT'S IN A NAME?

JULIET: *What's in a name? That which we call a rose*
By any other word would smell as sweet. . . .
. . . Romeo, doff thy name
And for that name, which is no part of thee,
Take all myself.

ROMEO: *I take thee at thy word.*
Call me but love, and I'll be new baptiz'd. . . .
—ROMEO AND JULIET (II, ii), 43 ff.

*O*F *COURSE,* names are mere labels and should have no part in love.

But they do.

For Romeo, the problem was not his first name (Juliet fudged this part a little), but his last: as a Montague, he was a sworn enemy of her family, the Capulets. In Shakespeare's Verona, that social enmity—plus his tendency to act first, think later—escalates from mischief to misunderstanding, malevolence, mayhem, what our judicial system calls second-degree murder, and a wrenching mistake that provokes the most famous double suicide in literature.

Yet, as Romeo said it would, his name became synonymous with love: four hundred years later, it is not uncommon in sweet, vulnerable moments for a woman of any age to call the man she loves MY ROMEO, MY SWEET ROMEO. Nor need we stop there: playing the lover's name game is a satisfying pursuit among the mutually entranced, be they languorously couchant or rampantly panting.

Who's on first in the love name game? Mom and Dad, that's who. Long before romance, sex, and all the affection we can sandwich in between rearranges our emotional constellations, there are parents: they choose what the world will call us. More often than we might suspect, it's a name that literally means love. Why they should label us as Love itself is unclear. A private remembrance of passion past? A job description for the ideal child? Or the fearsome hope of this stanza in Anne Ridler's "Choosing a Name":

> I love, not knowing what I love,
>> I give, though ignorant for whom
>> The history and power of a name.
> I conjure with it, like a novice
>> Summoning unknown spirits: answering me
>> You take the word, and tame it.

Even in these egalitarian, politically correct days there are more love names for girls than for boys—who are more likely to go through life answering to names that iterate people, places, or propaganda. Some of the many girl love names include ADORA and AMANDA, from Latin. CHARITY, from the Latin *caritas,* means "brotherly love," and MABEL, a name that has fallen out of favor in recent decades, comes from the Latin word for "lovable." JAIME is from the French *J'aime,* "I love." (It is also a feminine spelling for JAMES, an English form of JACOB, a name that means "supplanter" and ranks as a "love name" only for second wives or second-born children.) DODIE means love in Hebrew, KALILA in Arabic, KAMA in Sanskrit (from the name of the Hindu god of love), QUERIDA in Spanish and TAFFY and CARYN in Welsh. From sea to shining sea, Far East to Far West, Sikkim to Siberia, in ancient times and today, names like these abound on the birth certificates of baby girls. Equating girls with love is a trend that never dies, a universal, multicultural, historically resonant fact of sexual politics and affection.

A name like CORDELIA will please those who dote on word puzzles as well as beloved daughters: it's an anagram for "ideal heart" in two languages: the Latin *cor* for "heart," and *delia,* a rearrangement of the letters in "ideal." If King Lear had thought twice about his daughters' names, would he have disowned Cordelia and rewarded Goneril, whose awkward, singular name—I find no other Gonerils in literature or name lists—sounds uncomfortably like gonorrhea (a word known in Shakespeare's time)?

Some given names carry a powerful love message even

when the connection is only symbolic. HADASSAH, a Hebrew name, means "myrtle"—a symbol of Venus in ancient Greek myth. In the Biblical story, Hadassah was a Jewish orphan reared in Persia by her uncle; to protect her from anti-Semitism, he changed her name to Esther (which means "Persian Star," a poetic name for the planet Venus). When King Ahasuerus met her he was so smitten that he made her his chief consort; because of this relationship, she was able to save her people from the evil Haman, an event still celebrated by the Feast of Purim.

(Sometimes private associations intensify love associations. Long before I knew that Venus and myrtle went together, the name Myrtle had, for me, an aura of invincible, romantic, all-out but old-fashioned, female allure. My mother's Aunt Myrtle, one of six daughters born to a Frenchman and the granddaughter of a red-haired American stage actress, received 127 marriage proposals as a young woman. That she lived in a tiny corner of Arizona, with a population that never exceeded a few hundred, even on Saturday, only added to her legend.)

Baby boys are just as adorable as baby girls, and a few boys' names dare to say so. DAVID and JED mean "beloved" (in Hebrew), as do ALVIN (Old German), DARREL (French), KEVIN (Irish Gaelic), and LEIF (Scandinavian). ERASMUS, the name of the great humanist, means "lovable" (Greek). There are even two hotly impassioned boys' names: PRICE

(Welsh) means "son of the ardent one," and ARDEN (Latin) means "ardent."

If a baby doesn't receive a *nom d'amour* at birth, diminutives can usually do the trick. Affectionate add-ons at the tip of the tongue are -ELEH, -ETTA, -IE, -ISSA, -KINS, -OLA, and -Y. Another way to romance the given name is to give it a foreign accent: KATERINA or KATRINKA for Katherine or Kate, ANNABELLA for Ann, GIOVANNI for John. Perhaps because two lovers make a very tiny family together, even briefly, family-style nicknames seem to flourish, including infantile rhymes that are absurd under any other circumstances: DENNY-BENNY, for example.

Where parents leave off, lovers begin. Sometimes lovers give themselves entirely new names to celebrate the new people they feel they've become after falling in love. It's a practice that has nothing to do with intelligence or cleverness and everything to do with in-your-face ardor, divine dementia, and plain idiocy. These nicknames can be clever, but more often they are surprisingly dull—or maybe you have to be there.

Albert Einstein's early love was a young physicist named Mileva Maric; in their love letters, he was JOHNNIE, and she was DOLLIE. (In amorous relativity, $E=mc^2$, where E is *energy,* m is *mystery,* and c is *consensual.*) The tempestuous Isadora Duncan chose as a pet name for a lover who was also her theatrical manager the humdrum TOPSY. Nora Barnacle,

James Joyce's common-law wife, called him SIMPLEMINDED JIM. Émile Zola fared better: Jeanne Rozerot, his mistress and the mother of his two children, called him PRINCE CHARMING. (Maybe fairy tales do come true in France.)

Uncharming princes are regrettably more typical of modern times. According to the few hundred million or so royal gossips, the present Prince Charles of England calls his great and good friend Camilla Parker Bowles GLADYS and she calls him FRED. But wait! FREDERICK means "ruler in peace," and GLADYS, which has the word LADY in it, means "princess" in Celtic. Even better, a look into *The Dictionary of First Names* by name aficionados Leslie Dunkling and William Gosling informs us that GLADYS is Welsh (a natural for the Prince of Wales) and, as a name, "burst upon the scene" in the 1870s with a certain "exotic" sex appeal. (Still, a GLADYS is an iffy catch: it also means "small sword" in Latin.)

Though Diana (as of this writing, still the Princess of Wales) was reportedly not amused when she discovered, before her wedding to Charles, a bracelet engraved from FRED to GLADYS, she too has thrilled (or so it is said) to pet names. Amid the marital debris of the royal split in 1992 was the tape of an alleged conversation between the princess and an admirer who called her SQUIDGY.

For what it's worth, Charles's inclination toward loving pseudonyms is a royal tradition. Another Prince of Wales, later George IV, signed himself FLORIZEL in love notes to a woman called PERDITA, a stage actress named Mrs. Mary Darby Robinson (1758–1800). The future monarch first saw this particular inamorata on stage in Shakespeare's *A Winter's Tale,* where she played the lost princess Perdita, much in love with the dashing, heroic Prince Florizel.

Occasionally a proposed love name is strange in intent if not in actual utterance. In his autobiography *At Large with Huston and Hemingway,* writer Peter Viertal recalls Heming-

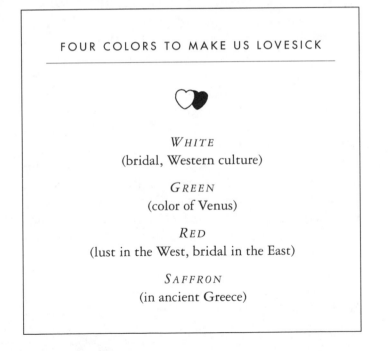

FOUR COLORS TO MAKE US LOVESICK

WHITE
(bridal, Western culture)

GREEN
(color of Venus)

RED
(lust in the West, bridal in the East)

SAFFRON
(in ancient Greece)

way's flirtation with Viertal's wife; among other things, this muddled venture included the bizarre suggestion, from a man nicknamed Papa, that should he and Viertal's wife have a daughter they could name her PETRA—a feminine form of Peter—"as a reminder of their fondness for me." Some love names supplant the original name officially. The historian Will Durant called his wife his ARIEL, after the more or less indentured spirit servant of Prospero in *The Tempest.* And that is the name she goes by as coauthor with her husband of several volumes in *The Story of Civilization* series.

With the confident insouciance of a man comfortable with women, Franklin Roosevelt called Eleanor BABS when they were young and MY MISSUS in later years. His successor, Harry S Truman, dubbed his wife, Bess, THE BOSS. Both husbands might be surprised to learn they were similar in these endearments to the rock star John Lennon, who called his wife, Yoko Ono, MOTHER and MADAM.

Jimmy Durante called his wife MRS. CALABASH. Louis Armstrong called Lucille Armstrong BROWN SUGAR, and George Burns still refers to Gracie Allen as GOOGIE, or KID. Carole Lombard and Clark Gable were young, beautiful, and had no children, yet she called him PA during their marriage, and he called her MA. (There is really no explaining this.) Years after Lombard's death, Gable and Grace Kelly had a romance; she called him BA, apparently modeled on the earlier love name, and, after the attraction faded, gave him a donkey named BA. (There is really no explaining this, either.)

It's not just Hollywood. The nineteenth-century English essayist and historian Thomas Carlyle and his wife, Jane, addressed each other with redundant enthusiasm as GOOD GOOD or GOODY; he also, in other moments, described her as his "necessary evil," and this devoted but cantankerous couple did best when they were apart and forced to communicate by letter. Apparently much happier were nineteenth-century English Prime Minister William Gladstone and Catherine Glynne—he the OAK and she the IVY—who were married for fifty-nine years.

What about the rest of us, lovers who star in one another's lives—and nowhere else? Nicknames are free, and we indulge just like everyone else. In fact, we wallow heedlessly, our intellectual senses suffused with private innuendo, incident, and (sometimes) over-the-line indecency.

It is a peculiarity of lovers that they often concoct endearments that sound like—and in fact *are*—insults. This is apparently permissible contempt bred of tolerant, allowable familiarity, a kind of testing. Like all exams, especially orals, it's tricky: you can't rewrite what you have already said out loud. Even the most loving relationships have awkward, edgy moments. Why exacerbate matters with sharp-tongued, potentially explosive, hurtful "endearments"? Because, lovers say, they don't really *mean* it . . . not *usually* . . . not the way it *sounds.* I suspect that we secretly savor such dangers, that we thrill to skirting the edge of feelings, because that's where passion flares.

Whatever the reason, loving insults are common. In the movie *On Golden Pond,* the wife refers repeatedly to her husband of many years as "you old poop," but even Katharine Hepburn, who won an Oscar for her performance opposite Henry Fonda, who also won an Oscar, as the aging husband, couldn't make this work, at least for me. Halfway through the film I was wondering if there was any legal precedent for justifiable strangulation, and if so, why didn't the Fonda character know about it?

Yet the following endearments are actual examples, used by acquaintances with their intimates: BASTARD, BITCH (or YOU LITTLE BITCH, "said slowly, and enunciated with affection"), CRYBABY, IDIOT (or DARLING IDIOT), FUSSPOT, PIZZA FACE, POOPHEAD, SCREAMER, SKINNY LIPS, SMARTASS.

Europeans fairly hum with insulting endearments. John Mortimer's fictional London barrister, Horace Rumpole, calls his wife SHE WHO MUST BE OBEYED. One real-life British family I know nicknamed a sister FEEB, short for "feeble." Cockney slang is full of rhyme, none flattering: CARVING KNIFE (wife), COWS AND KISSES (the missus), OLD POT AND PAN (old man or husband), and TROUBLE AND STRIFE (wife). In Dutch, loving insults get full play, espe-

cially in families: CHEESEHEAD (the Dutch term is
KAASKOPJE), CRAZY GUY, DIRT DEVIL, LITTLE STINKER, and
the classic SKUNKFOOT. Eastern European putdowns of af-
fection include (for children) PISHKIND, which is a combi-
nation of PISCH, Yiddish for "piss" and KIND, "child." In one
family I know, this has metamorphosed into the Spanish-
style PISHQUINATO.

Names are so personal, so intrinsic and individual, that it is
curious we should want to rename those who become our
one-and-onlys: why change what we find perfectly charm-
ing? But new, private names reinforce the strange, special
transport that love compels. They are secret codes that sig-
nal the shared fantasy of great love affairs.

The "real" name of the woman Don Quixote loves in Cer-
vantes's great comic novel, *Don Quixote,* is Aldonza Lorenzo,
a plain appellation for a plain, unremarkable woman de-
scribed by Sancho Panza, the faithful but realistic squire, as
"stout" and "sturdy." But to Quixote, Aldonza is the mag-
nificent DULCINEA DEL TOBOSO, a first name that means
sweetness and a last that smacks of aristocratic birth and
grand manners. It is a name that invokes Quixote's dream of
ideal female beauty, that suits the vision he sees when he
gazes upon her:

> *Her flowing hair is of gold, her forehead the Elysian
> fields, her eyebrows two celestial arches, her eyes a pair of*

glorious suns, her cheeks two beds of roses, her lips two coral portals that guard her teeth of Oriental pearl, her neck is alabaster, her hands are polished ivory, and her bosom whiter than the new-fallen snow.

We laugh at Don Quixote, but we know he does not lie.

LOVE LETTERS IN THE SAND

Wish you were here.

POSTCARD FROM SENATOR JOHN F. KENNEDY TO JACQUELINE BOUVIER,
REPORTEDLY THE COMPLETE TEXT OF HIS LOVE CORRESPONDENCE TO HER
DURING THEIR ENGAGEMENT

T'S ONE THING when
professional writers ply their trade and capture love on the
printed page: all they risk is poverty and humiliation. Love
letters, on the other hand, are for consenting *amateurs*—a
word that begins with love and applies even to professional
scribblers when they themselves fall victim to an excess of
amatory emotion.

A love letter tries to do the impossible: promise every-
thing eternally, describe desire, imprison passion, and com-
mit literally inexpressible, pulsing sensation to a flat, blank
sheet of paper. A good love letter does it so effectively that
the writer and the reader feel as if they are in each other's
presence again, if only for a moment.

The French call love letters BILLETS DOUX, "sweet notes";

American slang is franker but more energetic: MASH NOTES. Short or long, amatory epistles can be (and frequently are) laughable and idiotic when read by others or even one's own self, after the heat proves fleet. The fact is, love letters are risky business: they don't work, *they can't work,* if the magical forgiveness and understanding that go with love is absent. Worst of all, they have an annoying tendency to resurface—stuck into the pages of a book, slipped into an attic trunk—all too legible and revealing if and when things go sour.

In 1898, the French playwright Edmond Rostand wrote *Cyrano de Bergerac,* basing it on a seventeenth-century Frenchman of the same name. He didn't have to make up much: the real-life Cyrano was a superb fencer, a poet, a verifiable hero. But everything costs, and the larger-than-life Cyrano had a larger-than-life nose—a flaw that he considered major, even though his skill with the sword slashed the number of guffaws he had to endure.

In the play, Cyrano loves the beautiful and pure Roxane, but refuses to court her: he fears that she will reject him because of his nose, and his own exquisite sense of proportion rejects the idea of linking her beauty to his homeliness. Enter the dull, incredibly inarticulate, but very handsome Christian, who also falls in love with sweet Roxane. Christian turns to his friend for help in wooing Roxane, and Cyrano delivers in fine heroic style: he puts his own love for Roxane into words—mostly in passionate, perfectly phrased

love letters, sometimes in whispered asides—and passes
them on to Christian. But he can't resist soliciting Roxane's
opinion of the letters:

> CYRANO: [*Twisting his moustache*] He . . . writes
> well?
>
> ROXANE: Wonderfully. Listen now. [*Reciting as from
> memory*]
> "Take my heart; I shall have it all the
> more;
> Plucking the flowers, we keep the plant
> in bloom—"
> Well?
>
> CYRANO: Pooh!
>
> ROXANE: And this:
>   "Knowing you have in store
> More heart to give than I to find heart-
> room—"
>
> CYRANO: First he has too much, then too little; just
> How much heart does he need?
>
> ROXANE: You are teasing me!
> You are jealous!
>
> CYRANO: [*Startled*] Jealous?
>
> ROXANE: Of his poetry—
> You poets are like that . . .
>   And these last lines
> Are they not the last word in tenderness?

"There is no more to say: only believe
That unto you my whole heart gives one
cry,
And writing, writes down more than you
receive;
Sending you kisses through my finger-
tips—
Lady, O read my letter with your lips!"

—*EDMOND ROSTAND,* CYRANO DE
BERGERAC, *III, i, English verse
translation by Brian Hooker*

Pitching woo in love letters makes them tangible tokens of affection to hold, to remind, to reawaken, and to reassure. In the ephemeral world of feeling, letters are real. As proof of loving trust (however foolish), they are also material witness to one person's brave attempt to share private responses and perceptions with someone else—no small achievement in any age. As the future Supreme Court Justice Oliver Wendell Holmes wrote an *inamorata* (not his wife) at the turn of the century:

I have this moment received your most adorable letter. It is what I have been longing for & is water to my thirst. You say & do everything exactly as I should have dreamed. I shall keep it & when I am blue & you seem far away I shall take it out & read it & be happy again.

The most obvious danger that love letters pose is betrayal. An indiscreet letter accidentally or incautiously revealed can shake marriages and damage reputations. The next risk is more private. What if the recipient does not match the writer's passion, or worse, reads it and laughs? Worst of all, what if she tries a little blackmail? Holmes asked the woman to whom he sent this letter—one of at least 103 in a correspondence that lasted thirty years—to burn his missives. She didn't, and years later we can read of those moments when the noble jurist's probity went missing. One of Napoleon's love letters carelessly mentioned his troops' battle positions and, when intercepted by enemy generals, led to defeat. (Such were the "niceties" of war in those days that, after reading the letter and planning a new strategy, the enemy general sent it on its lovelorn way to the recipient, Madame Bonaparte.)

Love letters are as idiosyncratic as their writers, and embellishments count. Sir Winston and Lady Clementine Churchill, who called each other "Pig" and "Cat," decorated the margins of their letters with winsome drawings of cats and pigs. And then there's the envelope. Long before she ever met my father, my very proper, properly proportioned mother received a letter from an admirer addressed to "Miss Wigglebottom." Her father was enraged.

Many couples develop private codes within their personal dialect of love. The parents of a businessman I know always ended their letters to one another with the letters and numbers "Y.O. 143." Translation: "Yours Only, I Love You" (the numbers correspond with the number of letters in each word of "I Love You"). Codes flourish during war, although soldiers' preoccupations are not always as sweet; slang expert Paul Beale has compiled a number of lovers' acronyms popular among servicemen during times of war, when letters are censored. A sample:

SWALK. Sealed With A Loving Kiss, from the shorter SWAK (Sealed With A Kiss). SWANK is Sealed With A Nice Kiss. SWALCAKWS is Sealed With A Lick 'Cos A Kiss Won't Stick.

BOLTOP. *X* and *0* are short for *kiss* and *hug,* and the letters BOLTOP, over an X, stand for Better On Lips Than On Paper.

ILUVM. I Love You Very Much.

A number of geographically based love acronyms date from the two world wars in this century:

ITALY. I Trust And Love You
BURMA. Be Undressed and Ready, My Angel
NORWICH. [K]Nickers Off Ready When I Come Home
HOLLAND. Here Our Love Lies And Never Dies
EGYPT. Eager to Grab Your Pretty Tits (or Toes, as the case may be)

As a symbol, the nunlike LILY stands for chastity, innocence, and purity. As an acronym, it is proud redundancy for

"Lover I Love You," a nice bit of word play if the woman happens to have the name Susan, which in its Hebrew derivation means—aha!—Lily.

Jack Kennedy wasn't the only lover able to count his written love words on the fingers of one hand. A hundred and fifty years ago, a quick, hot exchange flew between the French actress Rachel (née Elisa Félix, the daughter of a peddler) and the man who became her great love, François d'Orléans, Prince de Joinville, third son of Louis Philippe. Seeing her perform one night, he sent his visiting card backstage with three words scrawled across it:

> *Où? —Quand?—Combien?*
> *(Where?—When?—How much?)*

Her reply:

> *Chez toi—ce soir—pour rien.*
> *(At your place—tonight—for nothing.)*

Equally impassioned if longer is this letter from the seventeenth-century French courtesan Ninon de Lenclos to the Marquis de Sévigné, who had left her side for a few hours:

> *Love! I feel thy divine frenzy! My trouble, my transports, everything announces thy presence—Today a new sun rises for me; everything lives, everything is animated, everything seems to speak to me of my passion, everything invites me to cherish it. . . . Since I love you, my friends*

*are dearer to me; I love myself more; the sounds of my the-
orbo and of my lute seem more moving, my voice more har-
monious. If I want to perform a piece, passion &
enthusiasm seize me; the disturbance they cause interrupts
me every minute. Then a profound reverie, full of delight,
succeeds my transports. You are present to my eyes; I see
you, I speak to you, I tell you that I love you. . . . I con-
gratulate myself and I repent; I wish for you, I wish to fly
from you; I write to you and tear up my letters. I reread
yours; they seem to me now gallant, now tender, rarely
passionate and always too short. I consult my mirrors, I
question my women about my charms. In brief, I love you;
I am mad; and I do not know what I shall become, if you
do not keep your word with me this evening.*

If the closest you've been to a love letter lately is a note
stuck on the refrigerator reminding you to take out the
garbage, it's time for a refresher course. Some of the letter
writers who follow are famous: overachievers often write
great love letters because loving without fear of embarrass-
ment can be a measure of a man or woman's personal confi-
dence and energy (er . . . make that egotism). The ones that
will break your heart come from those who lived ordinary,
often difficult, otherwise unsung lives—and who rose tri-
umphantly to an epistolary occasion.

TEN RULES OF LOVE-LETTER COMPOSITION

RULE 1: Write when you most miss the loved one.

Often this is immediately after you have been together. Kings don't usually have to write love letters, and they are blessed with protectors, known to the modern age as public-relations people, who dispose of (or save for their own memoirs) the tender *mots* of those they serve. Henry VIII addressed the following letter to Anne Boleyn, the young flirt for whom he reinvented English religion—a process that, not coincidentally, freed him to divorce Catherine of Aragon, marry Anne, and welcome the future Elizabeth I into the world as a child born on the "right" side of the sheets (that is, in wedlock). Like others in the first ecstasies of love, he found his perception of time strangely altered.

> *Myne awne Sweetheart, this shall be to advertise you of the great ellingness {loneliness} that I find here since your departing, for I ensure you, me thinketh the Tyme longer since your departing now last than I was wont to do a whole Fortnight; I think your Kindness and my Fervence of Love causeth it, for otherwise I wolde not thought it possible, that for so little a while it should have grieved me, but now that I am comeing toward you, me thinketh my Pains by half released, and also I am right well comforted, insomuch that my Book maketh substantially for*

my Matter, in writing whereof I have spent about IIII Hours this Day, which caused me now write the shorter Letter to you at this Tyme, because of some Payne in my Head, wishing my self (specially an Evening) in my Sweethearts Armes whose pritty Duckys I trust shortly to kisse. Writne with the Hand of him that was, is, and shall be yours by his will,

H.R.

GREAT LOVE WRITERS

THE CLASSICS: *Sappho, Ovid, Catullus*

OUR MEDIEVAL BEST: *Chaucer*

RENAISSANCE MEN: *Petrarch, Ariosto, Shakespeare, Sir Philip Sidney, Edmund Spenser, John Donne, Robert Herrick, Andrew Marvell*

RAUNCH THAT RHYMES: *John Wilmot,*
Earl of Rochester

PASSIONATE PROSE: *D. H. Lawrence, Emily*
and Charlotte Brontë, Gustave Flaubert, Ernest
Hemingway, Sidonie Gabrielle Colette, James
Joyce, Margaret Mitchell

TRUE ROMANTICS: *George Gordon, Lord*
Byron; Percy Bysshe Shelley; John Keats

ENRAPTURED RATIONALISTS: *Elizabeth*
Barrett, Robert Browning

AMERICAN EXTREMISTS: *Emily Dickinson,*
Edgar Allan Poe

MODERN SOPHISTICATE: *Vladimir Nabokov*

STEAMY SPECIALISTS: *Anne Rice, Erica Jong*

RULE 2: Answer immediately, and at length.

Love letters impress two ways—with the turn of delicate
phrase, and the weight of envelope. The twelfth-century let-

ters of Héloïse and Abelard are among the most passionate and sincere in any language; they may also be the longest. Though married, these two did much of their loving by mail, and they remained emotionally obsessed with each other for years. As Abelard wrote: "In the midst of my retirement I sigh, I weep, I pine, I speak the dear name of Héloïse, and delight to hear the sound." In this very brief excerpt, Héloïse tells Abelard what his letters mean to her:

> *Letters were first invented for consoling such solitary wretches as myself. Having lost the substantial pleasures of seeing and possessing you, I shall in some measure compensate this loss by the satisfaction I shall find in your writing. There I shall read your most sacred thoughts; I shall carry them always about with me, I shall kiss them every moment; . . . I had rather read the dictates of the heart than of the brain. I cannot live if you will not tell me that you still love me. . . . Vice never inspires anything like this: it is too much enslaved to the body. . . . I will still love you with all the tenderness of my soul till the last moment of my life. If, formerly, my affection for you was not so pure, if in those days both mind and body loved you, I often told you even then that I was more pleased with possessing your heart than with any other happiness, and the man was the thing I least valued in you.*

The "man" was Héloïse's pretty euphemism for testicles and lovemaking, and on the whole her renunciation of the flesh

was a nice try: Abelard had been castrated by thugs on the
direct order of Héloïse's uncle, and it was following that ter-
rible event that their long correspondence began. Here is a
part (a teensy-weensy snippet) of Abelard's reply:

> *If my passion has been put under a restraint my thoughts
> yet run free. I promise myself that I will forget you, and
> yet cannot think of it without loving you. . . . I inces-
> santly seek for you in my mind; I recall your image in my
> memory, and in different disquietudes I betray and con-
> tradict myself. I hate you! I love you! . . . I have ex-
> hausted my strength in constant exercises; I comment upon
> Saint Paul; I contend with Aristotle: in short, I do all I
> used to do before I loved you, but all in vain: nothing can
> be successful that opposes you.*

RULE 3: Don't claim to be what you aren't.

As Cyrano discovered, it is not a good idea to misrepresent
oneself—or someone else—in a love letter. Subterfuge defies
and ridicules trust, and phoniness swells past pretension to
give the lie to everything it touches, including the love it
celebrates. A hundred years ago the prolific critic, philoso-
pher, and playwright George Bernard Shaw enjoyed a
twenty-five-year affair of the heart with the actress Ellen
Terry. They never met: she feared she'd disappoint. Shaw
was a vegetarian, and George Jean Nathan, an American
drama critic, called their romance "a vegetarian amour—a

game of epistolary post office." But Shaw defended their paper passion: "Remember that only on paper has humanity yet achieved glory, beauty, truth, knowledge, virtue, and abiding love." As an actress, Terry was a professional pretender, but in her love letters she was without pretense.

> *18 September 1896*
> *Savoy Hotel*
>
> *I'm not good at knives and curses, but better at flying to lovers and enduring a good deal in the way of rocks and shocks.*
>
> *What are* you *best at?*
> *You seem to do everything.*
>
> *But I remember you made me laugh, and amused me more than I was ever amused, when I saw Arms and the Man. . . .*
>
> *You have become a habit with me, Sir, and each morning before breakfast,* I take you, *like a dear pill!*

In answer, Shaw was gallant, a tease, and very much his own person:

> *Up to the time I was 29, actually twenty-nine, I was too shabby for any woman to tolerate me. I stalked about in a decaying green coat, cuffs trimmed with the scissors, terrible boots, and so on. Then I got a job to do and bought a suit of clothes with the proceeds. A lady immediately invited me to tea, threw her arms round me, and said she*

adored me. I permitted her to adore, being intensely curi-
ous on the subject. Never having regarded myself as an
attractive man, I was surprised; but I kept up appear-
ances successfully. Since that time, whenever I have been
left alone in a room with a female, she has invariably
thrown her arms round me and declared she adored me. It
is fate. Therefore beware. If you allow yourself to be left
alone with me for a single moment, you will certainly
throw your arms round me and declare you adore me.

RULE 4: Set loose the child within.

Napoleon Bonaparte adored women almost as much he
lusted after power and glory. In love letters he lavished pet
names on the objects of his desire and wrote frankly about
sex: a letter to his wife Josephine advises that he will be
home in three days and tells her, "Don't wash." He was
playful as well as lecherous; this man had no fear of being
called silly, at least by the women in his life. His letters
seem carelessly composed, indifferent to structure, but
whether consciously or not he was a master of the unsubtle
allusion, as in this letter to Josephine.

Verona, November 13, 1796
I don't love you, not at all; on the contrary, I detest you—
You're a naughty, gawky, foolish Cinderella. You never
write me; you don't love your husband; you know what

pleasure your letters give him, and yet you haven't written him six lines, dashed off casually!

What do you do all day, Madame? What is the affair so important as to leave you no time to write to your devoted lover? What affection stifles and puts to one side the love, the tender and constant love you promised him? Of what sort can be that marvelous being, that new lover who absorbs every moment, tyrannizes over your days, and prevents your giving any attention to your husband? Josephine, take care! Some fine night, the doors will be broken open, and there I'll be. . . .

I hope before long to crush you in my arms and cover you with a million kisses burning as though beneath the equator.

Bonaparte

RULE 4A: When all else fails, make submission a patriotic duty.

Remember the Victorian mother's advice to her daughter, the night before her wedding, about sex? "Just close your eyes and think of England," she said. When Napoleon's love for Josephine waned, he sought the bed of Countess Marie Walewska, a Polish noblewoman. Three letters culminating in patriotic blackmail survive.

Jan. 1807

I have seen only you, I have admired only you, I desire only you. A very prompt reply to calm the impatient ardor of

N.

Have I displeased you? I hoped the opposite. Or has your first feeling vanished? My passion grows. You rob me of my rest. Vouchsafe a little joy, a little happiness, to the poor heart that would fain worship you! Is it so hard to give me an answer? You now owe me two.

{N.}

There are moments in life when high position is a heavy burden. That is borne in on me at this moment. . . . If only you would! None but you can overcome the obstacles which separate us. My friend Duroc will do what he can to make it easy for you. Oh, come, come! All your wishes shall be fulfilled! Your country will be even dearer to me, if you have compassion on my heart.

N.

RULE 5: If chiding lacks chic in your circle, consider (if you dare) the charms of logic.

Reason defies love, but it sounds impressive. In 1910, Bertrand Russell—English philosopher, mathematician, and social theorist—fell hard for Lady Ottoline Morrell, a London socialite. Both were married, she to a prominent politician. Does the philosopher's attempt to organize passion into numbered debate points make him more or less convincing as a lover? Does the proliferation of the word "I" help or hinder his romantic cause?

Now I will make up an exact statement, and please keep it in mind however dumb I may be, because it is at all times true.

1. I want to keep you and I want not to ruin your life. . . . Compared to these two, all other things in life are trivial to me. Don't doubt this.

2. I want to accomplish, during my life, a good deal more work in philosophy. . . .

3. I want to write general things on religion and morals and popular philosophy. I could do this even if I were discredited, because I could publish anonymously. I can imagine a sermon on Strife . . . and innumerable things of that sort.

4. I like teaching, but that is inessential.

I have put these four in order of importance, the most important first. . . . Whatever may be involved in our holding to each other, the harm to me will be less than if we parted. I believe seriously that the spring of life would be broken in me if we parted. . . . If I have you, there are other goods that may be added; if I don't have you, there are no other goods. . . . I have never imagined such love. I have had the feeling too that I ought to keep it back from you, so as not to interfere with your freedom—but I can't.

. . . With you there is life and joy and peace and all good
things—away from you there is turmoil and anguish and
blank despair.

Quiz Question: If you were Lady Ottoline, would you throw
everything over for this pretentious, presumptuous, pontifi-
cating, self-appointed prince of love? No? Well, neither did
she.

RULE 6: When Rules 4 and 5 fail, try sublime incoherence.

John Jay Chapman was born during the United States Civil
War and lived to see Hitler rise to power in Germany. A
New York lawyer at a time when lawyers were not always
confused with sharks, he also wrote essays and poems. In
love, Chapman went way beyond passion: once, to punish
himself for having beaten a man he (wrongly) thought had
bothered his sweetheart Minna Timmins, he stuck the hand
that did the beating into a fire "until the charred knuckles
and finger bones were exposed." He went to the hospital,
"showed the trouble to a surgeon, was put under ether, and
the next morning waked up without the hand and very
calm in [his] spirits." In time he married Minna, to whom
he wrote this perfect love letter:

{Postmarked Littleton, Colorado, September 21, 1892}
I have sealed up each one of these letters thinking I had
done—and then a wave of happiness has come over me—

remembering you—only you, my Minna—and the joy of life. Where were you, since the beginning of the world? But now you are here, about me in every space, room, sunlight, with your heart and arms and the light of your soul—and the strong vigor, your presence. . . . If we should sin—or separate—if we should fail or succeed— we have tasted of happiness—we must be written in the book of the blessed. We have had what life could give, we have eaten of the tree of knowledge, we have known—we have been in the mystery of the universe.

Is love a hand or a foot—is it a picture or a poem or a fireside—is it a compact or a permission or eagles that meet in the clouds—No, no, no, no. It is light and heat and hand and foot and ego. If I take the wings of the morning and remain in the uttermost parts of the sea, there art thou also—He descended into Hell and on the third day rose again—and there art thou also—in the list or business—in the stumbling and dry places, in sickness and health—every sort of sickness there also—what matter is it what else the world contains—if you only are in every part of it? I can find no corner of it without you . . . there was our great love over us, growing, spreading—I wonder we do not shine—or speak with every gesture and accent giving messages from the infinite—like a Sibyl of Michael Angelo. I wonder people do not look after us in the street as if they had seen an angel.

Tuo Giovanni

(Minna Chapman's note, written across the envelope: "La miraculosa littera d'amore"—the miraculous letter of love.)

RULE 7: When separated and having a good time anyway, criticize new acquaintances of the opposite sex.

After ten years of marriage and children, the poet William Wordsworth went, alone, to London. His letters to his wife, Mary, are full of gossip and awash with genuine sentiment and insistent, eager passion. They include this account of a dinner party:

> . . . and there I had the honour of being introduced to the Princess Regent; an empty honour, for her R.H—— was at some distance from me, and I had no conversation with her. She is a fat unwieldy Woman, but has rather a handsome & pleasing Countenance, with an expression of hilarity that is not however free from Coarseness. This was a large Assembly, saw few pretty women, and many more disgusting objects; one I encountered of a tolerable face & feature, but in her native bosom so huge & tremendous, that had you seen her enter a room in that condition I am sure the soul of modest womanhood in you would have shrunk almost as with horror. Her Breasts were like two great hay-cocks or rather hay stacks, protruding themselves upon the Spectator, and yet no body seemed to notice them— . . . But enough adieu my darling; a thousand kisses and embraces long & tender! . . .
>
> Thy faithful Husband W. W.

RULE 8: Be sincere and respectful.

During the great European migrations to the United States at the turn of the century, thousands of immigrants struggled to find their way in a new country without familiar rules, rituals, and—in the matter of marriage—matchmakers. A collection of useful letters, carefully preserved by Marlene Robinson of Scarsdale, New York, helped many Jewish arrivals. It was written in Hebrew, translated into English, and bound in books that read back to front. The publishing data has been lost from the book, but Robinson guesses, from the dates on some of the letters, that it first appeared in 1896. Tucked in among the necessary business letters were these two—and lucky the lover who happened upon them!

"DECLARATION OF LOVE TO A YOUNG LADY OF
LONG ACQUAINTANCE"

Cincinnati, O., Oct. 15, 18—.

My dear Miss Rosie,—

From my constantly meeting with you, and observing the many acts of amiability and kindness which adorn your daily life, I have gradually associated my hopes of future happiness with the chance of possessing you as their sharer. Believe me, dear Miss Rosie, this is no outbreak of boyish passion, but the hearty and healthy result of a long

*and affectionate study of your disposition. It is love,
founded on esteem; and I feel persuaded that your knowl-
edge of my own character will lead you to trace my mo-
tives to their right source.*

*May I, then, implore you to consult your own heart,
and should I not have been mistaken in the happy belief
that my feelings are in some measure reciprocated, to grant
me permission to mention the matter to your parents.*

*Believe me, dear Miss Rosie,
your ever sincere friend,
Alexander Loveman*

And: "Same Gentleman on Receiving a Favorable Answer"

Cincinnati, O., Oct.16, 18——.

*Dearest Rosie,——Words cannot express my delight on
finding your note on my table last night. The toils of the
day were over, but how delightful was it to find a let-
ter—and such a letter!—from one whom I may now hope
to hail as the companion of my whole future life! The
weight taken off my mind by the candid and gentle con-
fession of one whose love seemed too great a happiness to
hope for is beyond description. To-morrow I shall hasten
to the presence of her from whom I hope I may never hence-
forth be parted. I could not retire to rest without express-*

*ing my delight at finding that hopes so flattering have not
been in vain.*

> *Believe me, dearest,*
> *your devoted and happy lover,*
> *Alexander*

RULE 9: Say what your lover wants to hear about himself or
herself.

If your lover is a businesswoman, wax euphoric over her
bottom line. If he's a tennis pro, make the most of his
stroking. If a writer, ask to read her stuff—out loud, to
savor the syllables, to nurture the nuance. The great French
actress Sarah Bernhardt was shameless and forthright in tak-
ing lovers; one she pursued, and remained close to for years,
was the playwright Victorien Sardou. The following is an
undated letter to him:

Wonderful Boy,

*Where are you tonight? Your letter came only an hour
ago—cruel hour—I had hoped you would spend it with
me here.*

*Paris is a morgue without you: before I knew you, it
was Paris, and I thought it heaven; but now it is a vast
desert of desolation and loneliness. It is like the face of a
clock, bereft of its hands.*

All the pictures that hung in my memory before I knew

you have faded and given place to our radiant moment together.

Now I cannot live apart from you—your words, even though bitter—dispel all the cares of the world and make me happy; my art has been suckled by them and softly rocked in their tender cradle; they are as necessary to me now as sunlight and air.

I am as hungry for them as for food. I am thirsty for them, and my thirst is overwhelming. Your words are my food, your breath my wine. You are everything to me.

Your Sarah

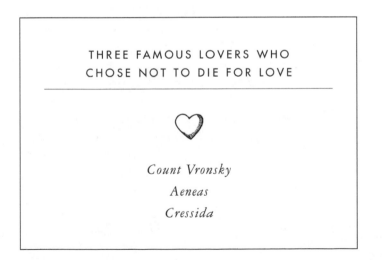

THREE FAMOUS LOVERS WHO
CHOSE NOT TO DIE FOR LOVE

Count Vronsky
Aeneas
Cressida

RULE 10: Trust yourself to say it perfectly.

For many, the most moving passage in the 1990 public television broadcast of *The Civil War,* the brainchild of documentary filmmaker Ken Burns, was this letter from a Union soldier to his wife before the Battle of Bull Run in Manassas, Virginia. He died a week later.

July 14, 1861   Camp Clark, Washington
My very dear Sarah,

    The indications are very strong that we shall move in a few days—perhaps tomorrow. Lest I should not be able to write again, I feel impelled to write a few lines that may fall under your eye when I shall be no more. . . .

    Sarah my love for you is deathless, it seems to bind me with mighty cables that nothing but Omnipotence could break; and yet my love of Country comes over me like a strong wind and bears me unresistibly on with all these chains to the battle field.

    The memories of the blissful moments I have spent with you come creeping over me, and I feel most gratified to God and to you that I have enjoyed them so long. And how hard it is for me to give them up and burn to ashes the hopes of future years when, God willing, we might still have lived and loved together, and seen our sons grown up to honorable manhood, around us. I have, I know, but few and small claims upon Divine Providence, but something whispers to me—perhaps it is the wafted prayer of my little Edgar, that I shall return to my loved ones unharmed. If I do not my dear Sarah, never forget how much I love you, and when my last breath escapes me on the battle field, it will whisper your name. Forgive my many faults, and the many pains I have caused you. How thoughtless and foolish I have often times been! How gladly would I wash out with my tears every little spot upon your happiness. . . .

But, O Sarah! if the dead can come back to this earth and float unseen around those they loved, I shall always be near you; in the gladdest days and in the darkest nights . . . always, always, and if there be a soft breeze upon your cheek, it shall be my breath, as the cool air fans your throbbing temple, it shall be my spirit passing by. Sarah do not mourn me dead; think I am gone and wait for thee, for we shall meet again.

THE GREATEST LOVE LETTERS OF ALL

Who wrote the greatest love letters? Besides our own sweethearts, that is?

Tastes vary. What titillates one woman may appall her

roommate. One man's mush may be the next man's manna from heaven. Yet I'd nominate the long correspondence of Sir Winston and Lady Clementine Churchill, a mighty bridge of love words that spans decades of devotion.

The Churchills wrote hundreds of letters and notes to each other for three reasons. They were often separated because of his political career, they took separate vacations, and they were rarely awake and alert at the same time—she was a morning person, he a night owl. (Is there a message here about how to have a happy marriage?) She was his "Kat" or "Cat," his "v[er]y wise and sagacious pussycat"; he was her "Pug," "Amber Pug," and finally "Pig." During her first pregnancy, they named their unborn baby "Puppy Kitten," or "P.K." After the birth of this child, who *ex utero* took the name of Diana, he wrote:

> . . . *try to gather your strength. Don't spend it as it comes. Let it accumulate. . . . My darling I so want your life to be a full & sweet one, I want it to be worthy of all the beauties of your nature. I am so much centered in my politics, that I often feel I must be a dull companion, to anyone who is not in the trade too. It gives me so much joy to make you happy—& often wish I were more various in my topics.*

Occasionally, in the early years of their marriage, she feared that his frequent absences meant he desired other women. His written response:

> *You ought to trust me for I do not love & will never love any woman in the world but you and my chief desire is to link myself to you week by week by bonds which shall ever become more intimate & profound. Beloved I kiss your memory—your sweetness & beauty have cast a glory upon my life. You will find me always your loving & devoted husband, W.*

Clementine was hot-tempered and fearless. But once, after a quarrel, she wrote him:

> *My sweet and Dear Pig, when I am a withered old woman how miserable I shall be if I have disturbed your life & troubled your spirit by my temper. Do not cease to love me. I could not do without it. If no one loves me, instead of being a Cat with teeth & Claws, but you will admit soft fur, I shall become like the prickly porcupine outside, & inside so raw & unhappy.*

These two Victorians had no trouble acknowledging physical desire. Several times during his service in France during World War I, Churchill got leave and was able to steal some private moments with his wife. Once they were almost late returning to Victoria Station. She wrote: "I could not tell you how much I wanted you at the station. I was so out of breath with running for the train." On the occasion of their tenth wedding anniversary, he wrote her:

> *Ten years ago my beautiful white pussy cat you came to me. They have certainly been the happiest years of my life, & never at any moment did I feel more profoundly & eternally attached to you. I do hope & pray that looking back you will not feel regrets. If you do it {is} my fault & the fault of those that made me. I am grateful beyond words to you for all you have given me. My sweet darling, I love you v{er}y dearly.*

Bravo.

TWENTY WAYS
TO LEAVE YOUR
LOVER

OSMETIC KING CHARLES REVSON gave his wife a gold chain dotted with diamonds for her birthday—the day before his lawyers served her with divorce papers. Loni Anderson says (or so say scribblers in the tabloid press) that Burt Reynolds told her he loved her—the night before he served her with divorce papers. As moderns, they got off easy, compared to the ancients we love to hate. If the televised version of Robert Graves's novel *I, Claudius* has it right, the ancient Roman emperor Caligula lusted for his favorite sister, Drusilla, and said so publicly— right up to the moment he served her with divorce papers in his own idiosyncratic way: he murdered her.

Breaking up is hard to do: popular singer Neil Sedaka made it to the hit list not once but twice with a song titled just that. It doesn't matter how regretful we feel: before, during, and after regret comes anger. The flip side of rapture can be as passionate, and as heartfelt, as the lovey-dovey good times; people who insist they no longer care for each other will argue for days in their lawyers' offices over who gets the cracked punch bowl. Some of it is a matter of pride: we do not like to be CUT DEAD, CUT OFF, DROPPED, DUMPED, THROWN OUT, or THROWN OVER.

The preferred GET LOST verb these days is SPLIT, but nothing so well communicates the jolt of separation as JILT. Dictionaries define this word (which always reminds me of *gilt* without "U" to qualify the meaning, a golden color or "superficial brilliance") as "to drop a lover capriciously or unfeelingly." It dates to 1673, and it works as a noun, too: a JILT is the one who does the capricious deed with little or no regard for finer feelings. In slang, JILT was, until about 1930, something more, less, and somehow much the same: as a verb, it meant to sneak into a building with the intention of robbing it, and as a noun it was the crowbar, a "housebreaking tool," that thieves used to gain entry. No wonder we say lovers STEAL HEARTS.

No one likes to get a DEAR JOHN LETTER, the slang term of World War II for the horribly cordial epistle a woman sent her soldier boyfriend when absence made the heart grow indifferent. In the *Dictionary of American Slang* (eighth edition), Paul Beale cites a song popular in the 1950s that included these charming lines: *Dear John, Oh, how I hate to write. . . . I'm to wed another, dear John.*

We check into the HEARTBREAK HOTEL for any number

TWO ESPECIALLY SUCCESSFUL
SERIAL LOVERS, FICTION

The Wife of Bath
Travis McGee

BONUS FOR DOUBLES:
TWO REAL MEN WHO LOVED AND LOST

Cyrano de Bergerac
Oscar Wilde

of good and bad reasons. Too often, familiarity breeds contempt. So do jealousy, greed, self-absorption, duty, and infidelity—even though we swore at the starting line that nothing would ever pull us apart.

Times change. Too bad.

Like many things in American life, the process of saying good-bye can be put in baseball terms. All red-blooded citizens who have attained sixth-grade level know the great baseball metaphor for sex: getting to first, second, and third base before sliding into home plate. The infinitely more complicated process of breaking up demands that we take the metaphor deep into the outfield and up into the stands. So whenever and wherever love dies, when there's no hope to KISS AND MAKE UP and it's painfully clear that you've been LOOKING FOR LOVE IN ALL THE WRONG PLACES, when even your cats know that THE PARTY'S OVER and decide it's safe to use his side of the closet as a litter box, here is a list of twenty classic, contemptuous, and contemporary ways to leave your lover and GET BACK INTO THINGS or INTO CIRCULATION.

WARMING UP IN THE BULLPEN

1. Hey, you've changed.
2. Hey, I've changed.
3. You don't really know me.
4. I want a divorce.

SACRIFICE FLIES

5. I'm no good for you.
6. You're too good for me.

GETTING TO FIRST BASE

7. This was a mistake from the beginning.

MAKING IT TO SECOND

8. Here's your hat, what's your hurry?

STEALING THIRD

9. There's someone else.

FOUL BALLS

10. Get lost.
11. Drop dead.

SLIDING HOME

12. But I want us always to be friends. Really.
13. I'm sure you'll make someone very happy someday.
14. "Your terrestrial envelope does not interest me, but does mine you?" (This dismissal was actually penned, toward the end of the nineteenth-century, by Marie Bashkirtseff, an upper-class Russian woman, to the novelist Guy de Maupassant, with whom she had corresponded under the alias "Miss Hastings." She terminated the flirtatious exchange without ever revealing her true identity. This final letter, which must to him have seemed almost alarmingly indifferent, is tempered somewhat in our eyes since we know, as he did not, that she was mortally ill: she died of tuberculosis at the age of twenty-four.)

CHOOSING AND SINGING THE ANTHEM

15. "You've Lost That Lovin' Feelin' "
16. "Hit the Road, Jack (And Don't You Come Back No More, No More, No More, No More)"
17. "Bye-bye, Baby, Good-bye"

AND UP IN THE PRESS BOX

18. "Frankly, my dear, I don't give a damn." (Margaret Mitchell wrote most of this short line in *Gone With the Wind;* Clark Gable made it sing when he ad-libbed the quintessentially dismissive "Frankly.")
19. "Get thee to a nunnery!" Shakespeare, *Hamlet.*
20. "Liar and cheat! . . . tigresses tendered their teats to you. . . . I hope and pray that on some grinding reef/ Midway at sea you'll drink your punishment. . . . I shall be everywhere/ A shade to haunt you! You will pay for this, Unconscionable! . . ." (Dido to Aeneas in the *Aeneid*—here from Robert Fitzgerald's luminous translation—when he announces that he has tarried by her voluptuous and generous side long enough and must now leave for Italy, where he's scheduled to establish a new civilization.)

Are these suggestions gratuitously cruel? Yes and no. It's important, if love dies, to let the other person know that IT'S ALL OVER, DONE, KAPUT, FINISHED. This can be conveyed in reasonable, polite terms apparently: we've all heard of the FRIENDLY DIVORCE, although I, for one, have never met one. Frankly, overly civilized, imprecise, or vaguely worded letdowns suggest two things to me: either the dropper doesn't want the droppee to think ill of him or her, which is asking more than a reasonable person should; or maybe the dropper isn't really sure what he or she wants. Of course, no one welcomes the possibility of being hated, loathed, despised, contemned, excoriated, detested, or even shrugged off. But I think love is so important, so essential, so much a thing to be valued that we should give its endings the same intense scrutiny and respect that we give its beginnings—with this proviso: unlike the verbal excesses of love in bloom, in separation the less we elaborate the more likely we are to exit with skin intact.

Alas, even when the decision to part is sincere and clearly stated, some lovers don't—or won't—get the message. At such times, strong language can sometimes make the point stick. In 1924, E. B. White broke off an ebbing romance with a young woman named Alice Burchfield. His letter was, in my opinion, brutal. But it is honest, and it decisively put to an end a relationship that was becoming increasingly dishonest—something that seems antithetical to White's character.

> *We weren't friends, so the friendly letters were flivvers.*
> *The strange part is that you failed to discover how ridicu-*
> *lous I was a long while ago. You even answered the let-*

ters. You mustn't forget that. I hope I'm not being more blunt than's necessary, but I don't want misunderstanding to run along any further. When I saw you last fall, it seemed to me that any doubts which you might have had concerning my "status" (if you want to call it that) were cleared up. I certainly talked about the weather. And then I began to receive letters from you saying that you were tearing up your initial attempts. I wasn't too dense to comprehend—but I don't think you realized that I did comprehend. . . . You see, you (and not I) were the one who continued to row after the boat had sunk.

Both White and Miss Burchfield survived their encounter and married—she to a college classmate, James F. Sumner, and he (caught in an incandescent lifetime love) to Katherine S. Angell.

CONCLUSION
The Last Word on Love

*L*OVE IS what we make it. So is language.

The language of love is emotional, not rational. It is personal, idiosyncratic, slippery, and generally unmanageable. It demands luck, perseverance, and sincere devotion. Love words can soothe and annoy, create and destroy. Lovers will use language, however approximate and inadequate, to define their emotional priorities and make their own rules. Those we love, and the ways we love them, say more about us as individuals than anything else.

Our evolutionary advantages as human beings are an opposable thumb, a big brain, and speech. The first allows us to use tools; the second gives us the ability to make those tools ever more complex; and the third enables us to go, with or without tools, into any area of interest. Language is a way of identifying and exploring new emotional landscapes.

The most mysterious territory is that of the heart. Words allow us to put our feelings into words, or try to; we can explain ourselves, and take stabs at denotative meaning on a very connotative subject. Except for the whales, who produce lengthy sonar songs of the deep that *may* be conversation (for all our opposable thumbs, note taking, and general cleverness, we have not been able to decipher them), no other animal can so expand vocally upon the infinite varieties and shades of feeling.

It doesn't matter that with so many words at our disposal, and so much heartfelt intention, we rarely (if ever) get it quite right: that is part of love's mystery. What counts is that we put this very human gift, this blessing of language that is as unwieldy and brilliant and necessary as love itself, to the task. The language of love is caring made audible, affection spoken aloud or written in permanent ink for all time. It makes a difference.

For years one of my good friends was a woman who was perpetually sad. She functioned well, she was intellectually curious, and she knew how to laugh. She had a solid marriage, and she cared very much about her loved ones—children, parents, siblings, friends. But always there was an unhappy, unsatisfied side to her, an aura of melancholy.

One evening, when our families were together for a holiday dinner, I was trying to pass a dish to my husband, who, in the general clamor, did not hear my sweetly lisped, dulcet, attention-getting calls. Finally I raised my voice: "Hello, my angel, my hero, my dearest, I love you more than I can say but if you don't take this platter off my hands my wrist is going to break and I will be very annoyed."

My friend watched us with obvious amazement, and the conversation turned to the subject of endearments.

"Well, yes, sometimes I tell the children 'I love you,' " she said slowly. "But my husband and I—it's understood, of course, but we never *say* it to each other." In fact, as I knew from our many lunches together, sometimes she and her husband went weeks and months without saying *anything* to each other.

Was the sadness that seemed to hover about her due, at least in some part, to the absence of verbal love play, to the fact that apparently by mutual consent she and her husband eschewed the murmured exchange of sweet talk? I am not a marriage counselor or a psychiatrist; I know better than to give my opinion about the inner workings of someone else's marriage. My friend was a complex, sophisticated woman very sure of her own and her husband's devotion, however mute. But I wondered then, and I still do, if life would have been more joyous for her if she had been able to revel in the delicious reinforcement of self-worth that love language— freely given, without hesitation, without fear of reproof or embarrassment—bestows. I wondered if this woman, who was herself gifted in the use of language, would have been gayer if she'd been able to use her verbal talents to give and return compliments in kind, to celebrate affection and family and, yes, passion.

This book offers dozens of love terms and endearments, but even the simplest converse between two people who care for each other can convey affection. Another couple I know has been in love since they were teenagers. Through four children and numerous relocations, educations, and career changes, they seem never to have doubted each other, or to have stopped regarding each other with open and sweet affection.

"We call each other 'sweetheart' and 'honey bunch' and say 'I love you' to each other a lot," my friend says. They say "Have a good day" and "Take care" often; they sign notes and letters to one another with Xs and Os for kisses and hugs.

"We are very close and talk about everything in great depth, but I think we try hard not to unnecessarily hurt each other's feelings or wound self-esteem," she adds. "I would say that the language of our love is true courtesy to each other, lots of 'pleases' and many 'thank yous,' and expressions of concern if one of us is very stressed or not feeling well physically, and sincere apologies if we have been short with each other."

Language of any kind is communication; love language is a constant affirmation of intimate, personal connections. One gentleman I know, a man on whom that sobriquet is not wasted, has been married for more than fifty years to a woman he quite frankly adores. To others she is formidable, reliable, and decisively, unromantically straightforward. To him she is his "darling girl," his "sweet," his "most precious." This year he celebrates his ninety-second birthday.

Every morning my friend reaffirms his abiding, uncritical love by making his wife breakfast and taking it to her in bed. And every morning, when she rises and takes her plate to the kitchen, she finds a message waiting on the counter, spelled out in toothpicks:

I LOVE YOU

Chaucer, the first great love poet in English, wrote that LOVE IS BLIND; the idea was that even though Cupid (the baby godling of love) is blind, the arrows he shoots invariably find their mark. That must be why lovers so often overlook or simply do not see the flaws, apparent weirdness, or plain ugliness of those who enchant them. In our more recent idiom, they LOOK THROUGH ROSE-COLORED GLASSES, which means that everything they see has a warm, flattering glow.

Maybe love has to be blind, or at least marginally distorted, to work—so much of it depends on shared fantasy. In fact and in fiction, happy lovers are willing to perceive each other in the best light, to recognize and respond to their best selves, to fulfill their strongest, most joyous potential. This is what romance—that emotional, essential state triggered by lust and refined by idealism—is all about. The territory where fact and fantasy merge is strange and marvelous (that is, full of marvels). As Joseph Wood Krutch, an American theater critic and scholar, observed, "Love is, then, not a fact in nature of which we become aware, but rather a creation of the human imagination."

As I am well aware. To use some of the giddier, more adolescent language in this book, I think that my husband is "drop-dead gorgeous." I have said, and I stand by it, that he is what an Italian Robert Redford would look like, if he (the Italian Robert Redford) were lucky. My husband scoffs; he says I am "crazy." My friends smile tolerantly, pat me on the shoulder, and assure me that he is a "nice"-looking man. As it happens, he thinks I'm "gorgeous" too. I don't think he's "crazy," not exactly, but I feel grateful, amused, delighted (and immensely relieved that this inexplicable lapse in logic and judgment in an otherwise level-headed man does not plague him in other parts of his life).

The most important thing to remember about love language is that it works: it heals, it binds, it reinforces, it comforts. Failure to use it can mean trouble, plunge unrequited lovers into misery, and even provoke disaster. Consider this familiar problem described in Mozart's opera *The Magic Flute* (here described in program notes by Charles Rizzuto for the New York Metropolitan Opera): "Having taken Tamino's silence for indifference, Pamina is in despair and on the verge of suicide."

Of course, sometimes there are good reasons not to speak

of love. The moment may be inappropriate, the timing premature. Usually lovers fail to tell one another of their passion because they fear it will not be returned. There can be real danger in speaking too soon: the smitten can blow their chances for later, when the ones they love might "come around"; they can look or feel foolish; they can wind up nursing damaged feelings. This may be what the literary critic Yvor Winters was referring to when he described the "crowded terror" that is love.

Well, yes: private feelings are tender and easily crowded; lovers can be cruel. The American playwright Lillian Hellman once described talk of love as "jabber," and much of the love language in this book is language not "run amok," exactly, but certainly listing toward laughable. Even, I admit, edging past embarrassment and falling flat into foolishness. I've heard tell that one bit of male-to-male advice on the subject of love is "Never talk in bed."

It's a familiar sentiment. In a poem from 1793—titled "Love's Secret" by David Perkins, editor of *English Romantic Writers,* and "Never Seek to Tell Thy Love" by Oxford scholar Helen Gardner—William Blake warned in pretty rhyme that speaking of love ruins it (text from Perkins):

> *Never seek to tell thy love,*
> *Love that never told can be;*
> *For the gentle wind does move*
> *Silently, invisibly.*

I told my love, I told my love,
I told her all my heart;
Trembling, cold, in ghastly fears,
Ah! she doth depart.

Soon as she was gone from me
A traveller came by
Silently, invisibly—
He took her with a sigh.

But in the long run it is better, I think, to offer love than to withhold it; better to express love freely than to measure it out in teaspoons; better to risk waving its banner overhead than to clutch it so close to the chest that it passes unnoticed and uncelebrated. In love, as in many things, Chaucer knew it all; in *Troilus and Criseyde* he wrote, "For he that naught n' assaieth, naught n' acheveth."

Or, as Sir William Schwenck Gilbert, half of Gilbert and Sullivan, wrote in *Iolanthe:*

Faint heart never won fair lady!
Nothing venture, nothing win—
Blood is thick, but water's thin—
In for a penny, in for a pound—
It's love that makes the world go round!

Or as we say today: no pain, no gain.

So speak up in love. Use the gift of language to acknowledge and understand the gift of passionate feeling. Words enable us to communicate what we feel as well as what we know, and feelings—however touchy or uncertain or overwhelming—are everything in love. Language can testify to our good will and high regard; language is a bridge of faith. Love words are the vocabulary of romance, the regional dialect of intimacy. William Blake wrote in one of his many short songs: "There is love: I hear his tongue."

So may we all hear it, and soon, and again.

BIBLIOGRAPHY

Edited and translated works:

The Aeneid, trans. by Robert Fitzgerald. New York: Random House, 1983.

A Book of Love Poetry, ed. by Jon Stallworthy. New York: Oxford University Press, 1973.

Chaucer, Geoffrey. *The Works of Geoffrey Chaucer, 2nd Ed.* Ed. by F. N. Robinson. Boston: Houghton Mifflin Company, 1957.

Cervantes Saavedra, Miguel de. *Don Quixote,* abridged and ed. by Lester G. Crocker. New York: Washington Square Press, 1957, 1963.

Dante. *The Inferno,* trans. by John Ciardi. New York: A Mentor Book published by the Penguin Group, 1954, 1982.

John Donne: The Complete English Poems, ed. by A. J. Smith. New York: Penguin Books, 1971.

English Romantic Writers, ed. by David Perkins. New York: Harcourt, Brace & World, Inc., 1967.

The Iliad: Homer, trans. by Robert Fitzgerald. New York: Anchor Books, Doubleday, 1974. Reissued by Knopf, distributed by Random House, 1992.

The Language of Flowers, ed. by Sheila Pickles. New York: Harmony Books, 1989.

Letters of E. B. White, ed. by Dorothy Lobrano Guth. New York: Harper & Row, 1976.

Nothing but the Marvelous: Wisdoms of Henry Miller, ed. by Blair Fielding. Santa Barbara, California: Capra Press, 1991.

The Odyssey: Homer, trans. by Robert Fitzgerald. New York: Vintage Classic Series, Random House, 1990.

Ovid's Amores, trans. by Guy Lee. New York: The Viking Press, 1968.

Ovid: The Metamorphoses, trans. by Horace Gregory. New York: A Mentor Book, New American Library, 1958.

The Riverside Shakespeare, textual ed. G. Blakemore Evans. Boston: Houghton Mifflin Company, 1974.

Dictionaries, compilations, and encyclopedias:

The American Heritage Dictionary of the English Language, 3rd Ed. Boston, New York: Houghton Mifflin Company, 1992.

Aphrodisiacs: An Encyclopedia of Erotic Wisdom. [No author.] London: The Hamlyn Publishing Group Limited, 1990.

Banned: Classical Erotica, compiled by Victor Gulotta and Brandon Toropov. Holbrook, Massachusetts: Bob Adams, Inc., Publishers, 1992.

The Best Baby Name Book by Bruce Lansky. Deephaven, MN: Meadowbrook, Inc., 1991.

Billboard's Hottest Hot 100 Hits: Facts and Figures about Rock's Top Songs and Song Makers by Fred Bronson. New York: Watson-Guptill, 1991.

Brewer's Dictionary of Phrase and Fable, Centenary Edition, rev. ed. by Ivor H. Evans. New York: Harper & Row, 1981.

The Cambridge Encyclopedia of Language by David Crystal. Cambridge: Press Syndicate of the University of Cambridge, 1987.

The Concise Columbia Dictionary of Quotations by Robert Andrews. New York: Avon Books, 1987, 1989.

A Dictionary of American Idioms, 2nd. ed., by Adam Makkai. New York: Barron's Educational Series, 1987.

A Dictionary of Slang and Unconventional English: Colloquialisms and Catch-phrases, Solecisms and Catachreses, Nicknames and Vulgarisms by Eric Partridge, ed. by Paul Beale, 8th Edition. New York: Macmillan Publishing Company, 1984.

The Dictionary of Historic Nicknames by Carl Sifakis. New York: Facts on File Publications, 1984.

The Dictionary of Imaginary Places, expanded ed., by Alberto Manguel and Gianni Guadalupi. Toronto, Ontario: Lester & Orpen Dennys, Publishers, 1987.

Dictionary of Problem Words and Expresssions by Harry Shaw. New York: McGraw-Hill Book Company, 1975.

A Dictionary of Symbols by J. E. Cirlot, trans. from Spanish by Jack Sage. New York: Dorset Press, 1971.

Dictionary of Word and Phrase Origins, Vol. II., by William & Mary Morris. New York: Harper & Row, 1966.

Dictionary of Word Origins by Jospeh T. Shipley. New York: Philosophical Library, 1945.

Essential American Idioms by Richard Spears. Lincolnwood, Ill.: National Textbook Company, 1990.

The Facts on File Dictionary of First Names by Leslie Dunkling and William Gosling. New York: Facts on File Publications, 1983.

Familiar Quotations by John Bartlett, ed. by Emily Morison Beck *et al.,* Boston, 15th and 125th anniversary ed. Boston: Little, Brown and Company, 1990.

Fifty Famous Letters of History, ed. Curtis Gavin Gentry. New York: Thomas Y. Crowell, 1930.

Forbidden American English by Richard A. Spears. Lincolnwood, Ill.: Passport Books, a div. of NTC Publishing Group, 1990.

Fowler's Modern English Usage, 2nd ed., rev. and ed. by Sir Ernest Gowers. Oxford and New York: Oxford University Press, 1983, 1984.

Funk & Wagnalls Standard Handbook of Synonyms, Antonyms & Prepositions by James C. Fernald. New York: Funk & Wagnall's, 1947.

Gardener's Latin: A Lexicon by Bill Neal. Chapel Hill, North Carolina: Algonquin Books, 1992.

Immortal Poems of the English Language: An Anthology, ed. by Oscar Williams. New York: Pocket Books, Simon & Schuster, 1952.

The Insomniac's Dictionary: The Last Word on the Odd Word by Paul Hellweg. New York: Facts on File Publications, 1986.

Kind Words: A Thesaurus of Euphemisms by Judith S. Neaman and Carole G. Silver. New York: Facts on File Publications, 1983.

Knock on Wood & Other Superstitions by Carole Potter. New York: Bonanza Books, Sammis Publishing Company, 1983.

The Little Brown Book of Anecdotes, ed. by Clifton Fadiman. Boston: Little, Brown and Company, 1985.

The Love Letters of William and Mary Wordsworth, ed. by Beth Darlington. Ithaca, N.Y.: Cornell University Press, 1981.

The Lover's Quotation Book: A Literary Companion, ed. by Helen Handley. Stamford, Connecticut: Pushcart Press, 1986.

Le Mot Juste: A Dictionary of Classical & Foreign Words and Phrases.

Vintage Books ed. panel. New York: Vintage Books, 1980, 1981.

New Dictionary of American Slang by Robert Chapman. New York: Harper & Row, 1986.

The New Oxford Book of English Verse, 1250–1950, ed. by Helen Gardner. New York and Oxford: Oxford University Press, 1972.

The Oxford Classical Dictionary, 2nd Ed., ed. by N. G. L. Hammond and H.H. Scullard. Oxford: Clarendon Press, 1970.

The Oxford Companion to Popular Music by Peter Gammond. Oxford, New York: Oxford University Press, 1993.

The Oxford English Dictionary. Oxford: Oxford University Press, 1971.

The Oxter English Dictionary: Uncommon Words Used by Uncommonly Good Writers by George Stone Saussy III. New York: Facts on File Publications, 1984.

The Penguin Dictionary of Modern Humorous Quotations, comp. by Fred Metcalf. New York: Penguin Books, 1986.

The Penguin Dictionary of Quotations by J. M. and M. J. Cohen. New York: Penguin Books, 1960.

The Reader's Encyclopedia, 2nd Ed., ed. William Rose Benet. New York: Thomas Y. Crowell Company, 1965.

A Second Treasury of the World's Greatest Letters, ed. Wallace Brockway. New York: Simon & Schuster, 1941.

The Selected Letters of Bertrand Russell, Volume I: The Private Years, ed. Nicholas Griffin. New York: Houghton Mifflin Company, 1992.

Slang! The Topic-by-Topic Dictionary of Contemporary American Lingoes by Paul Dickson. New York: Pocket Books, Simon & Schuster, 1990.

Smaller Classical Dictionary by Sir William Smith, rev. by E. H. Blakeney and John Warrington. New York: E. P. Dutton & Co., Inc., 1958.

A Treasury of the World's Great Letters, ed. Max Lincoln Schuster. New York: Simon & Schuster, 1940.

Understanding British English by Margaret E. Moore. New York: Citadel Press, Carol Publishing Group, 1989.

The Viking Book of Aphorisms: A Personal Selection, ed. W. H. Auden and Louis Kronenberger. New York: Dorset Press, Viking Press, 1962, 1966.

Webster's Ninth New Collegiate Dictionary. Springfield, Mass.: Merriam-Webster, Inc., 1984.

Words: A Connoisseur's Collection of Old and New, Weird and Wonderful, Useful and Outlandish by Paul Dickson. New York: Dell Publishing Co., 1982.

Other books and publications:

Agel, Jerome and Walter D. Glanze. *Cleopatra's Nose: The Twinkie Defense, and 1500 Other Verbal Shortcuts in Popular Parlance.* New York: Prentice Hall Press, 1990.

Berlitz, Charles. *Native Tongues.* New York: Perigee Books, pub. by The Putnam Publishing Group, 1982.

Brandreth, Gyles. *More Joy of Lex: A Celebration in Praise and Pun of the English Language.* New York: William Morrow and Company, Inc., 1982.

Brontë, Charlotte. *Jane Eyre.* New York: Signet Classic, New American Library Penguin, 1960.

Brontë, Emily. *Wuthering Heights.* New York: Signet Classic, Penguin Group, 1959.

Dolan, Edward F. *Animal Folklore.* New York: Ivy Books, Ballantine Books, 1992.

Durrell, Lawrence. *Clea.* New York: Penguin Books, 1966.

Farb, Peter. *Word Play: What Happens When People Talk.* New York: Alfred A. Knopf, 1974.

____. *Humankind.* Boston: Houghton Mifflin Company, 1978.

Feldman, David. *Who Put the Butter in Butterfly?* New York: Harper & Row, 1989.

Funk, Charles Earle. *Heavens to Betsy! and Other Curious Sayings.* New York: Perennial Library, Harper & Row, 1955.

____. *A Hog on Ice and Other Curious Expressions.* New York: Perennial Library, Harper & Row, 1948.

____. *Thereby Hangs a Tale: Stories of Curious Word Origins.* New York: Perennial Library, Harper & Row, 1950.

Funk, Wilfred. *Word Origins and their Romantic Stories.* New York: Grosset & Dunlap, 1950.

Graves, Robert. *I, Claudius.* New York: Vintage Books, 1934, 1961.

Hilton, Conrad. *Be My Guest.* New York: Prentice Hall Press, Simon & Schuster, 1957.

Joyce, James. *Ulysses.* New York: Vintage Books, Random House, 1961.

Jones, Julia, and Kenneth Ames. *Love Tokens.* Stamford, CT: Longmeadow Press, 1992.

Jung, Carl. *The Psychology of the Unconscious.* New York: Princeton University Press, 1943.

Kornstein, Daniel J. "Justice Holmes in Love," article in the New York State Bar *Journal,* July/August 1992.

Lawrence, D. H. *Lady Chatterley's Lover.* The Complete and Unexpurgated 1928 Orioli Edition. New York: Bantam Books, 1968.

Macrone, Michael. *Brush Up Your Shakespeare!* New York: Harper & Row, 1976.

Maleska, Eugene T. *A Pleasure in Words.* New York: A Fireside Book, Simon & Schuster, 1981.

Manchester, William. *The Last Lion: Winston Spencer Churchill: Visions of Glory, 1874–1932.* New York: Laurel, Bantam Doubleday Dell, 1983.

Martin, Ralph C. *Jennie: The Life of Lady Randolph Churchill.* Englewood Cliffs: Prentice-Hall, 1969–71.

McCullers, Carson. *The Member of the Wedding,* a play. New York: New Directions Publishing, 1949, 1951.

Laroque, Francois. *The Age of Shakespeare.* New York: Harry N. Abrams, Inc., 1993.

Lederer, Richard. *The Miracle of Language.* New York: Pocket Books, Simon & Schuster, 1991.

Mitchell, Margaret. *Gone With the Wind.* New York: Avon Books, 1973.

Muller, Marcia. *Where Echoes Live.* New York: The Mysterious Press, 1991.

Rees, Nigel. *The Phrase That Launched 1,000 Ships.* New York: A Laurel Book, Dell Publishing, 1991.

Rose, H. J. *Gods and Heroes of the Greeks.* Cleveland and New York: Meridian Books, World Publishing Company, 1958, 1963.

Schwartz, Kit. *The Female Member.* New York: St. Martin's Press, 1988.

____. *The Male Member.* New York: St. Martin's Press, 1985.

Sperling, Susan Kelz. *Lost Words of Love.* New York: Crown Publishing, 1993.

Streep, Peg. *A Gift of Herbs.* Watercolors by Claudia Karabaic Sargent. New York: Viking Studio Books, Viking Penguin, 1991.

Styron, William. *Sophie's Choice.* New York: Random House, 1979.

Thorn, Dr. Mark. *Taboo No More: The Phallus in Fact Fantasy and Fiction.* New York: Shapolsky Publishers, 1990.

Viertal, Peter. *Dangerous Friends.* New York: Doubleday, 1992.

Wallechinsky, David, and Irving Wallace. *The People's Almanac #3.* New York: Bantam, 1981.

Walson, Lillian Eichler. *Standard Book of Letter Writing and Correct Social Forms.* Englewood Cliffs, N.J.: Prentice-Hall, 1948, 1958.

Ward, Geoffrey C., writer, and Ken Burns, documentary filmmaker. *The Civil War,* public television stations, 1992.

Wayne, Jane Ellen. *Grace Kelly's Men.* New York: St. Martin's Press, 1991.

ABOUT THE AUTHOR

Susan Ferraro is a freelance writer for various periodicals. Originally from California, she earned her A.B. from the University of California, Berkeley, and was awarded an A.M. and a Ph.D. from Harvard University. She is the recent recipient of the Benita Feury Award, in recognition of her distinguished writing on breast cancer advocacy. She lives in the New York City area with her husband and their two children.

X O X O X O X O X O X O